PASTORAL

of the

ANOINTING OF THE SICK

by

Dr. Adolf Knauber
Universität-Professor, Freiburg im Breisgau

translated by

Matthew J. O'Connell

with discussion questions and the officially
approved provisional text of

RITE OF ANOINTING
and

PASTORAL CARE OF THE SICK

THE LITURGICAL PRESS
Collegeville   **Minnesota**

Fr Hite
Dec 75

PASTORAL THEOLOGY OF THE ANOINTING OF THE SICK is the authorized English version of Chapter 7, "Die Kranken und die Sterbenden in der Kirche," in *Handbuch der Pastoraltheologie*, Praktische Theologie der Kirche in ihrer Gegenwart, Band IV, herausgegeben von Franz Xaver Arnold, Ferdinand Klostermann, Karl Rahner, Viktor Schurr, Leonhard M. Weber; Verlag Herder, Freiburg im Breisgau.

Nihil obstat: William G. Heidt, O.S.B., S.T.D., *Censor deputatus. Imprimatur:* ✛ George H. Speltz, D.D., Bishop of St. Cloud. July 31, 1975.

Pages 1A–60A Copyright © 1975, The Order of St. Benedict, Collegeville, Minnesota.

ISBN 0-8146-0879-5

CONTENTS

PASTORAL THEOLOGY

of the

ANOINTING OF THE SICK

1. *Name and Interpretation*

Until Vatican Council II, the usual name for the sacrament of the sick was "Last Anointing."[1] The Council, however, officially provided another and "more fitting"[2] name: "Anointing of the Sick." The change thus introduced into the Church's linguistic usage has important consequences, the full extent of which we do not yet comprehend, for a new dogmatic and pastoral understanding of this much misinterpreted sacrament. Speaking of nos. 73–76 in the Constitution on the Sacred Liturgy,[3] the official commentator on the working text at the Council explained that the name "Anointing of the Sick" is preferable to "Last Anointing" because it clearly counteracts the idea, suggested to priests and faithful alike by the term "last," that "the sacrament should be received only in very great danger of death or even at the moment of dying." Ecclesiastical usage has consequently been altered, and the old name has finally disappeared from recent documents.[4]

Behind the shift in terminology, important insights drawn from the history of sacramental practice and from biblical and liturgical theology are at work. The name "last anointing" arose within the framework of the high medieval penitential discipline for the reconciliation of a dying penitent.[5] It became the ordinary name only at the end of the twelfth century; descriptions such as "oil of the sick," which had been current up to that time (and which persisted even to a later period), show that the sacrament had earlier been understood in a broader way.

It was, therefore, in the light of contemporary pastoral practice that the Scholastics developed the conception of the "sacrament of the dying." This unsatisfactory expression was then, unfortunately, taken up by the Council of Trent, although the Council's intention (as its omission of the evaluative adverb "rightly" from the text as originally proposed indicates) was simply to report the fact of its usage.[6] In a similar or even more non-committal way, the official Roman Catechism of the Council of Trent simply notes such names as being traditional.[7] A few years before, on the other hand, the Catechism of Friedrich Nausea, archbishop of Vienna, had sharply rejected the "sacrament of the dying" interpretation; this Catechism lists the "so-called last anointing of the sick" in seventh place in the sacramental series, but gives as the reason that this anointing is last in rank (not in time) among the five anointings practiced in the Church.[8]

Terminology based on medieval practice was unfortunately responsible for the spread of many unbalanced conceptions and for even more ill-advised theological catchwords, for example, "sacrament of the consecration for death," "sacrament of the resurrection," etc. These only increased the resistance which pastoral care for the sick has always encountered. All the more welcome, then, is the language of the most recent documents, which speak only of the sick, not of the dying. Success has finally crowned twenty years of effort to renew liturgical practice.[9] In the future it will not be permissible to characterize the anointing of the sick as "the sacrament of death,"[10] and the interpretation "consecration for death" (always in open contradiction to the very prayers used in this "consecration"!) is no longer acceptable.[11]

2. *Canonical Prescriptions*

Up to the present the relevant prescriptions of the Code of Canon Law (1918) and of the Roman Ritual (1614), which in turn reflected the decrees of Trent, have determined the rite for anointing the sick. The canons of Trent, however, were concerned only with the sacramentality of the anointing, its nature as mediation of grace, its Scriptural justification, and its administration by the hierarchic priesthood alone (canons 1–4). This means that any further determinations made by Code or Ritual are to be interpreted in the light of the pastoral practice of the time and of the Scholastic theology, which was itself conditioned by that practice.

This fact is important when it comes to the conditions required for valid reception and administration. In the Latin Church today, the anointing of the sick is administered only in case of serious illness or dangerous weakness due to age. Up to the present the norm for deciding when such conditions are present has been expressed in the phrase "danger of death"; but this concept is obscure from the viewpoints both of the history of medicine and of pastoral theology, and it has been the subject of sharp disagreements.[12] It can at least be said, however, that the phrase does not mean the death agony ("the point of death") nor primarily[13] and exclusively an especially acute or hopeless stage in the threat to life.[14]

It is true that Vatican II uses the hitherto customary phrase "danger of death" once in the Constitution on the Liturgy (no. 73), but the text explicitly says that the right moment for anointing the sick has already arrived when the poor health of the patient *begins* to be a threat to his life. In other words, at this point the probability that the sacrament may be administered is now a certainty. The sacrament may therefore legitimately be administered in any truly serious illness in which its symbolism as "medicine" can be meaningfully applied. Obviously, trivial sicknesses are not meant; but apart from this, no perfectly clear boundaries can be drawn in determining validity.[15] The only contraindicated cases are those of a person already certainly dead and of a person who certainly either lacks an at least virtual, faith-inspired intention to receive the sacrament or who has not reached the age of reason.

For the fully fruitful reception of the sacrament, an at least imperfect repentance is also required and, if there is serious sin, confession, to the extent that this is possible.

The olive used for the anointing, the solemn consecration of which on Holy Thursday has come to be reserved to the bishop (after the function of the concelebrating presbytery had lost its true meaning), may in the future be blessed in simple form by priests of the Latin rite, at least in cases of necessity[16]; previous canonical indults and approbations do not limit this permission.

The minister of the sacrament is the Ordinary and, after him, any priest. In anticipation of a possible future discipline, however, it must be said that, at least from the viewpoint of biblico-liturgical and dogmatico-pastoral tradition, there is no serious objection to an extraordinary empowering of other ministers by the hierarchy; only a special commission from the hierarchy is required.[17]

Finally, the repetition of the anointing,[18] all essential conditions being verified, seems not to be a matter affecting validity at all, even though such repetition was earlier rejected or accepted in only a limited degree; at most it is a matter of canonical legitimacy. In such cases, then, a sensible and healthy pastoral outlook must have the final say.[19]

Far more important than all these limitations imposed by the now questionable practice of the past will be a revitalized rite based on understanding of biblical and liturgical theology. Such a rite must make the power of the sacrament available in a better, that is, broader and more differentiated, way than has up to now been the case. This means, above all, the pastoral use of the normal *solemn form* in a truly liturgical celebration of the anointing of the sick, with the patient not yet in an acute stage of his illness. Such a solemn form would be distinct from a form for administration in case of necessity, that is, for the anointing of dying persons, which has unfortunately become, in practice, the usual occurrence; this latter form would be analogous to baptism or confirmation in case of necessity.

Too much stress ought not to be laid on the "continuous rite" required by the Constitution on the Liturgy (no. 74); such a requirement is aimed simply at reaffirming the objectively proper place of the anointing of the sick: after confession (if needed) and before Communion. Above all, such a continuous rite, with its provision for Viaticum, must not become a pretext for returning to the idea of the anointing of the sick as appropriate only in the final moments of life.

3. *The Liturgy of the Sacrament*

The liturgical celebration of the anointing of the sick has now happily been renewed, in accordance with the principles enunciated in the Constitution on the Liturgy (nos. 61–63), and its longstanding close connection with the medieval discipline for penance and death has finally been broken. Henceforth its texts and rites can "express more clearly the holy things which they signify" (Constitution on the Liturgy, no. 21; Abbott, p. 146). Beyond this, however, there is the further need that the two stages of the full liturgical rite, which have for centuries developed independently in the Western Church, be seen in unity: the *administration* of the sacrament and the *consecration of the oil of the sick*.

a) *Administration*

The anointing itself normally — that is, outside of an emergency — takes place within a larger symbolic framework.[20] In the ideal case it is, like baptism and confirmation (Constitution on the Liturgy, nos. 71 and 78), incorporated into a Mass celebrated either in the sick person's home or in a place of worship (for example, the chapel of a hospital or old people's home). When it is not celebrated within a Mass, special introductory and closing rites are provided. After an opening blessing at the door of the sickroom, accompanied by a friendly exhortation to the sick person and to the other participants in the celebration,[21] and after an opening prayer, a suitable short passage of Scripture is read. Next is a responsory prayer (litany or prayer of petition), which may or may not, according to circumstances, be prolonged by psalmody. At this point the communal "prayer of faith" (James 5:14) should give the whole rite the dimension of community activity. The penitential part of the rite, to be done in common, whether or not the patient makes his confession, also helps to give special expression to the communal aspect.

The nucleus of the sacramental celebration consists of the *priest's prayer* and the *anointing*. Extending his hands over the sick person,[22] the priest invokes Christ the Redeemer.[23] Should there be no oil available that has been solemnly blessed by the bishop, oil is blessed here in simple form. After the priest has prayed, he anoints the sick person's forehead and hands while reciting the revised sacramental formula. This formula, in keeping with the promise made in James, prays not only for the sick person's "forgiveness" but also for his "raising up" and "salvation." When done outside the celebration of Mass and Communion, the anointing of the sick has a closing rite with texts that "correspond with the varying conditions of the sick who receive the sacrament."[24] These lead to a concluding blessing.

b) *Consecration of the Oil*

The sacramental symbolism of the anointing of the sick is fully intelligible only if we see it in the light of the solemn consecration of the oil, which takes place on Holy Thursday in the Chrism Mass concelebrated by the bishop and his college of priests (just as the baptismal rite acquires its full depth of meaning only in the light of the Paschal Vigil). If, then, the blessing of the oil can be delegated to priests at other times, that is, of course, to be welcomed in the interests of a more widespread understanding of faith in this sacrament — provided that the blessing retains its place in the overall sacramental rite and is not downgraded to an obscure, out-of-the-way ceremony.

The texts for song and reading in the Chrism Mass, together with the Preface, concentrate on the old soteriological symbolism of "oil of anointing — anointing by the Spirit — participation in messianic salvation."[25] The oil of the sick is blessed at the altar itself and at the place in the Eucharistic Prayer that has been allotted to it since early times — just before the words "Through whom you create all these good things" which precede the solemn doxology at the end of the Canon. (The chrism and the oil of catechumens are blessed only at the end of Mass before the Prayer after Communion and at a table specially set up for the purpose.) The special symbolism of the "consecrated" oil of the sick, as distinct from the chrism and oil of catechumens, emerges impressively from the two prayers of blessing spoken over it. The first, an exorcism formula, prays that "this oil may have power to effect a spiritual anointing so that the temple of the living God may be strengthened and the Holy Spirit be able to dwell in it."[26]

The second prayer takes the form of a solemn epiclesis in which the Holy Spirit himself is invoked upon the oil. "Lord, we pray you, send your Holy Spirit, the Advocate, from heaven upon this olive oil . . . that it may strengthen soul and body and that by the power of your holy blessing anyone anointed with this heavenly medicine may be protected in soul and body and be freed of all pain, weakness, and sickness of soul and body." This central part of the epiclesis terminates in the invocational formula: "As you once anointed priests, kings, prophets, and martyrs, so may the perfect chrism which you have blessed for us continue to work within us."

This deeply meaningful prayer has had a checkered textual history. However, despite the numerous revisions it has undergone from the Gelasian Sacramentary to the present-day Pontifical, it still clearly reflects the earlier practice of a more liberal application of the "holy oil."[27] It is beyond doubt, moreover, that the clause "As you once anointed . . ." does not refer to the oil; in accordance with biblical idiom much used in an earlier day, it refers rather to the Holy Spirit who has just been invoked in the main part of the sentence.[28] It is also clear that the expression "your perfect chrism," with its allusive imagery, means the Holy Spirit, who is the crowning messianic gift to Christ and Christ's saving gift to us.[29]

What has been said indicates that from the viewpoint of liturgical theology, the anointing with oil, an ancient form of popular medicine, here becomes the external sacramental sign of a deeper salvation-event. Interiorly, the anointing with the Holy Spirit comes to the aid of the sick person as a "heavenly medicine" (Roman Ritual) which promises and effects relief of bodily and spiritual weakness and a new strength.[30] Such is the self-understanding of the rite itself and the interpretation of it given by the Council of Trent[31] and, in harmony with the Council, by the Roman Catechism.[32] Other interpretations often proposed,[33] such as "consecration for perseverance in the death struggle," "for final victory," "for the special state proper to the sick," "a revitalization of the anointing at confirmation" and others, can be justified neither by the formula of administration nor by the prayer texts.

The liturgical tradition of the anointing of the sick as such knows no express *prayers for the dying*. Throughout all the changes in text forms, the old prayers have always put the basic stress on "alleviation," "strengthening," and "healing."[34] It is really striking how, despite widespread practice based on extreme cases (so that the sacrament was administered only to the hopelessly ill), the prayers of the sacrament have always been for a return to health, restoration to customary activities, and reunion with the liturgical community.

Confident prayer along the lines intended and required by the Lord must continue to characterize the anointing of the sick. The Roman Catechism justifiably lays great stress on the fact that this is the only sacrament to be "brought into existence by numerous prayers." In other words, the sacrament is not administered here by a simple formula alone; the priest and the faithful present must with sincere zeal devote themselves to prayer for the life and health of the sick person.[35]

The liturgy for the anointing of the sick thus reflects with convincing fidelity the normative biblical instruction contained in the Letter of James.

4. *Scriptural Source*

James 5:14-16, "If one of you is ill . . ." (*Jerusalem Bible*), is the fundamental biblical text, and the priest recalls it when he prays at the administration of the anointing of the sick. In order to correctly understand this much disputed text,[36] its larger context must be noted: the Apostle is giving religious instruction on three different situations in the life of a member of the community (5:13-16). The concluding lesson is especially to be kept in mind: "So confess your sins to one another, and pray for one another, and this will cure you; the heartfelt prayer of a good man works very powerfully."

The special situation of the sick person (v. 14) is distinguished from those of the person who "is in trouble" (v. 13a) and of the person who "is feeling happy" (v. 13b). The latter is to sing a hymn of praise, the former must pray. Special instruction (v. 14) and special promises (v. 15) are then given to the sick person. The sick person being considered here is obviously someone forced to stay at home or perhaps even bedridden. Nothing is said, however, of imminent death or danger to life.

The sick person is to summon the "elders" of the community. These men, officials of the Church, will pray "over him," that is, not only for him but "directing their prayer toward him" (perhaps even: with hands extended over him, as in Origen's interpretation[37]), and simultaneously, or previously, anoint him with oil in the power of the Lord. This simple gesture was familiar to the contemporary religious mind, which associated sickness and demonic powers, on the one hand, and prayer and the Lord's saving power, on the other; the meaning of the gesture must have been immediately plain.[38] To it an effect is promised unconditionally: the prayer of faith will bring rescue (salvation) to the sick person; the Lord will raise him up, and forgiveness will be his if he has committed sins.[39]

The attempt has recently been made to give these three future-tense verbs a purely "eschatological" meaning, as though "will save" signified preservation from eternal death and "will raise up" signified resurrection from the

tomb. But such an interpretation ignores the concrete
situation envisaged in the text, which says nothing of a
dying person.[40] The future tense here indicates only logical consequence, that is, the immediate effect of the
prayer. On the other hand, the reference can hardly be to
a directly intended and sensibly observable medicinal
effect of the bodily order. The verbs "save" (v. 15) and
"heal" (v. 16) must refer rather to that "rescue" and "healing" which are proper to the situation of the sick person
as envisaged from the *religious* viewpoint — that is, the
healing of the religious powerlessness and spiritual
weakness that sickness causes, as well as of temptation
and difficulty in believing and trusting.

Consequently, we will be better advised not to interpret the three verbs in question as three successive and distinct effects: "bodily," "spiritual," and "supernatural."[41]
In Scripture the three verbs, after all, often refer con-
cretely to one and the same reality and are almost
identical. We should therefore take them in that broad
and non-specific, "unsophisticated and undifferentiated"[42] sense which they naturally have in the
special situation of a person lying ill in bed: he is to be
"raised up" from his weakness and "rescued" from the
dangers to salvation which his weakness entails. A "healing," in the sense of a directly intended, palpable,
guaranteed, quasi-charismatic liberation from bodily illness as such, cannot be meant here, given the larger context in James's letter. As the person in trouble is to pray
and the happy person is to sing songs of praise, so the sick
person is to summon the elders for the prayer of faith
(along with anointing and imposition of hands); thus each
person has his own proper way of mastering the situation
in which he finds himself.

It is from the *naturalness* with which the presbyteral
ministry, the "official" prayer of faith, is requested and
carried out, and from the *assurance* with which a salvific
effect on the sick man's condition is ascribed to the symbolic ecclesial action, that the Church derives the sacramentality of the anointing of the sick. Even though James

5:14-15 reports no express word of institution by the
Lord, it does attest to a rite that was already being practiced in apostolic times in a clearly official way and "in
the name of the Lord."[43]

5. *Historical Development of Pastoral Practice*

The practice and doctrine of anointing the sick have
had such a checkered development over the centuries
that it is possible to speak only within narrow limits of a
unified tradition. If, then, we desire to appreciate the sacrament in its true nature and to foster its full pastoral
development, we must carefully distinguish its substance
as grasped in biblical and liturgical theology from the
more accidental and historically conditioned forms it has
taken in the past.

Down to the Carolingian pastoral reform, the anointing
of the sick was a more or less unstructured and open sacramental mode of faith-inspired care for the sick in the
broadest sense of this term (First Phase).

From this turning point on (eighth-ninth centuries), the
anointing of the sick underwent, about every four
hundred years, numerous and varied shifts of emphasis.
In a first stage it onesidedly developed, for the clergy
involved in organized pastoral care, into an increasingly
obligatory liturgical rite for assisting the dying (Second
Phase).

This contemporary discipline became in turn the basis
for the theological speculations and varied theories of
early and high Scholasticism and its newly developed
sacramental theology (Third Phase).

Four hundred years later the Council of Trent attempted
not only to ward off the attacks of the Reformers, but also
to rectify the worst exaggerations of the medieval tendencies to deferment of the sacrament and to spiritualism.
Since, however, the emphasis in the doctrinal formulas of
Trent was determined by polemics against the Reformers,
the distorted stresses of the earlier period continued to be
effectively at work, even if below the surface (Fourth
Phase).

Only with the movement of liturgical renewal in our own time has it been possible to achieve a more thorough reflection on essential structures and to have Vatican Council II officially impose this on the Church (Fifth Phase).

First Phase of Development

The instructions in the Letter of James initially found little echo in the writings of the early Church;[44] rituals for the anointing of the sick are in evidence only from the eighth century on. In the earlier period the main concern of the faithful seems to have been the possession and personal use of the consecrated oil, which they themselves had brought to be blessed in church and then taken home with them. The solemn blessing by the bishop during Mass was initially regarded as the real ecclesial and sacramental factor.

In a culture in which anointings with oil were common in many sicknesses, the private use of oil consecrated "in the name of the Lord" was not felt to be contrary to James's instructions. We find this stated quite explicitly by Venerable Bede, even though in his time the stress was beginning to shift to the prayer of the priest who had been summoned to give aid and to the anointing which he administered.[45] The oldest consecratory prayers (Hippolytus, Serapion, the Gelasian and Gregorian Sacramentaries[46]) give the impression at a first reading that they regard the medical symptom of bodily healing as the primary or even exclusive effect of the oil of anointing.[47] But closer examination quickly shows that the numerous formulas which verbally deal with bodily health are expressing in fact a deeper intention that is concerned with the healing of man in his entirety: the prayers ask for strengthening and forgiveness of sin, for new vitality and protection for body, soul, and spirit.[48]

It is not permissible, then, to interpret such texts onesidedly as evidencing a grossly materialistic view of sacramental causality. The ultimately important thing in the texts is their religious and finalistic orientation; they are concerned, that is, with the situation of the sick man as a person in regard to salvation or damnation of soul and body, with the overcoming of demonic powers, and with the indwelling of the Holy Spirit and Christ's power — in a word, with expectations that are thoroughly soteriological and spiritual, not profane, in character. No wonder, then, that given the biblical and Christian background, the prayer of petition should express an expectation even of full bodily healing.

In any event, it is notable and significant that in this first period the oil of the sick seems to be utilizable by any Christian and in any form whatsoever ("anointing with it, tasting it, touching it"[49]), and that it may be used in any sickness and is not specifically limited to danger of death or proximate danger to life. This observation applies especially to the first main instance of a formal appeal to James's instructions, namely, the letter of Pope Innocent I (410) to Bishop Decentius of Gubbio in Umbria[50]; according to the Pope, the "Roman custom" is to be observed in the unrestricted administration of the sacrament (only the unreconciled sinner is to be refused).

Only in the seventh and eighth centuries does the role of the administering priest come to be stressed, especially by Venerable Bede, who appeals explicitly to the Gospel and to the apostolic instructions in James's letter.[51] Neither Bede nor his age knows of any restriction to the danger of death,[52] but there are already some signs of a link between the anointing of the sick and the rite of penance for the sick, of which the anointing will later be a regular part.[53] Up to this time "there seems to have been the practice of free charismatic improvisation"; now begins the period of "rites." At the end of the eighth century we suddenly find numerous texts with the title "Rite for visiting or anointing the sick."[54] A decisive change has occurred in the interval.

Second Phase of Development

After Charles the Great's inquiry into sacramental practice and the resultant episcopal reports and capitularies, ever more numerous pastoral instructions and rituals for the care of the sick made their appearance. In them the sacrament becomes, even if in somewhat differing ways, a set part of "penance at the time of death," and its administration in such cases becomes a duty of the clergy.[55] The very fact that the anointing of the sick was inserted into text-collections of rituals for practical use and that these comprehended in one volume all that was needed, from the imposition of penitential ashes and the use of penitential garb and the penitential psalms to be recited down to the commendation of the soul and at times even to the office of burial, could not but affect the understanding and pastoral esteem of the sacrament.[56]

Given the high mortality rate and frequent suddenness of death, pastoral care of the sick must often have been limited to quite simple provisions for the dying and the mortally ill. This became the normal case, and consequently what had been a *duty* for the clergy now became a *permission* for the people[57]; that is, recipients of the anointing of the sick had to be at death's door. A further factor was that since the anointing of the sick was closely connected with the strict penitential discipline — itself permitted, in practice, only once to each individual — it was delayed as long as possible by the faithful, that is, until death was inevitable. In this way they could minimize for themselves as much as possible the rigorous penitential requirements in respect to clothing, fasting, and continence in marriage; those who recovered had to observe these prescriptions for the rest of their lives.[58]

It was in this context that there arose not only the idea of the non-repeatability of the sacrament,[59] but also the no less questionable theological conception of the "consecration" given to the sick person by the anointing. A person who unexpectedly recovered was treated as a revenant from the other world, as one who was dead as far as this world was concerned; he might no longer raise his hand in an oath, use his feet for dancing, etc.[60] The deferring of the sacrament is here closely allied to an unhealthy spiritualism. At the end of the period these tendencies necessarily led to the idea of "last anointing" as "sacrament of the dying" — a very widely popular conception which found ready acceptance in medieval piety, since the latter was already narrowly concentrated on the "art of dying." In addition, from the viewpoint of pastoral and doctrinal theology, that same conception did a great deal of harm to the sacrament of the anointing of the sick and even had some effect on the liturgical texts.[61]

Third Phase of Development

In the course of the twelfth and thirteenth centuries, the practice we have been describing was increasingly translated into doctrinal principle. This led ultimately to a full speculative sanctioning of the practice by the great masters of high Scholasticism: St. Albert the Great, St. Thomas Aquinas, St. Bonaventure, and Duns Scotus. On the one hand, these men no longer had any living contact with the early liturgical tradition and with the Eastern Churches.[62] On the other, the new and flourishing theology of the sacraments was pushing them toward a categorization of ideas formed in early Scholasticism. The result was that the questions and categories of the School (matter and form, ultimate content [*res sacramenti*] and effect, performance of the rite [*opus operatum*] and causality, etc.) were applied to last anointing as it was known in the pastoral practice of the time, that is, as linked to the penitential discipline, with the danger of death as a condition for reception, with reservation of the blessing of oil to the bishop, and with the canonical restrictions on repetition and on administration to those under the age of discretion (*impuberes*).

The greatest difficulty for Scholastic speculation was the "medicinal" character of the sacrament. "Healing" as an (infallible!) effect of the sacrament could only be interpreted, it seemed, in a thoroughly spiritual sense. The original conception of a "means of healing" in a "bodily-spiritual" weakness (such as is present in every illness that attacks the human person in a serious way) had been completely lost. In any event, the spirituality of the age was not interested in man's mastery of his earthly situation, but was shaped by the idea of preparing for eternity. No wonder, then, that sacramental doctrine was primarily concerned with the eschatological dimension and that care of the sick, with its established triad of penance-Viaticum-last anointing, was understood precisely as *the* initiation into eternal life.[63]

The fundamental text on which all Scholastic reflection on the anointing of the sick is based and to which it refers as a norm is not taken from, e.g., the liturgy, but from the book on which all the Schoolmen commented: Peter Lombard, *Libri Sententiarum*, IV, d. 23. Peter gives the cue for all thinking about the sacrament, and no one ever questions its validity: "the anointing of the sick, which is administered in the final moments of life." Albert the Great restates this in the formula "sacrament of the dying" and draws the doctrinal conclusion: "This sacrament is never to be received except by the dying" (*In IV Sent.*, d. 23, a. 11).

In St. Thomas, this Albertine thesis has already become the basis for all further statements on the hierarchy of the sacraments and on the place of "last anointing": "This sacrament is the last remedy the Church can offer, and it all but immediately disposes the person for glory. This is why it is to be administered only to those sick persons who are dying" (*In IV Sent.*, d. 23, q. 2, a. 4, sol. 2). To the objection that all the sick require medicine, he answers: "But this sacrament's primary effect is the health required by those who are dying and on their way to glory" (*Summa theol.*, *Suppl.*, q. 32, a. 4, ad 2). St. Thomas considers both the name and the practice of "last anointing" to be a very old and unquestionable ecclesiastical tradition.[64]

Scholars have occasionally pointed out in St. Thomas the existence of formulations which betray a broader vision, and they have thought they discerned a development in his thought between the *Commentary on the*

Sentences and the *Contra Gentiles.* In fact, in *Contra Gentiles* St. Thomas does express an important idea about the connection between bodily weakness and sin: "Since the body is instrument of the soul . . . it is fitting that there be a spiritual medicine against sin, inasmuch as bodily weakness derives from sin" (IV, 73). In the conclusion of *Summa theol., Suppl.,* q. 30, a. 1, he comes even closer to a fundamentally correct understanding of the sacrament: "Since the sacrament effects what it signifies, we must judge the main effect of the sacrament by its symbolism. This sacrament is administered, in fact, the way any medicine is. . . . It follows that the sacrament was instituted chiefly to heal the weakness caused by sin." Unlike baptism and penance, the anointing of the sick is not directed against original sin and mortal sin as such, but against a certain "weakness and unfitness" arising from sin and affecting man spiritually so that "he does not have his full strength for the activities proper to the life of grace or glory."

Unfortunately, however — and the practice of his time and its "vital context"(*Sitz im Leben*) are to blame — St. Thomas interprets this lack of strength as the lack peculiar to the *end* of life, and the "strengthening" effected by the sacrament as exclusively eschatological, that is, as a preparation for the "life of glory." His basic outlook, therefore, remains unchanged: "It is clear, then, that this sacrament is the final one and that it is, in a sense, the crowning stage of all spiritual healing, for by it a man is prepared to share in God's glory" (*Contra Gent.* IV, 73). "The last anointing . . . removes the remnants of sin and makes a man ready for final glory" (*Summa theol.,* III, q. 65, a. 1). St. Thomas' *Commentary on the Creed,* written toward the end of his life, offers the same explanation.

St. Bonaventure and Duns Scotus draw even more restrictive conclusions from the pastoral practice of their time. "However sick a person be, he is not given this sacrament unless he can be presumed to be dying or is on the point of dying. If it be clear, on the contrary, that the person is being cured of his illness, he is not to receive the sacrament" (St. Bonaventure, *In IV Sent.*, d. 23, a. 1, q. 1, ad 1-2-3). Scotus is quite consistent in requiring as a disposition proper to this sacrament and as a presupposition of its effectiveness the extreme state in which the patient is no longer capable of even venial sin or of personal acts of penitence; in other words, he requires the death agony. He sees as the essential effect of the "last anointing" that the dying person is to enter blessedness, free of every sin (Scotus, *Reportata Parisiensia in IV Sent.*, d. 23, q. unica, n. 3; 16, no. 7, ad 2).[65]

In the theology of the high Middle Ages, our sacrament of the sick thus became the sacrament of final preparation and qualification for the vision of God. This complete eschatologization of the sacrament, with its serious pastoral consequences, also represents the final stage, more or less, in the doctrinaire process of deferring and spiritualizing the sacrament. If the resultant theology were to be interpreted as the official doctrine of the Church, the Greek Orthodox theologians would be right in accusing the Latin Church, ever since the *Dialogue* of Simeon of Thessalonica († 1429), of "falsification of doctrine" on the grounds that it "has transformed the sacrament of the healing of the sick into a sacrament of the dying."[66] Unfortunately, this kind of theology has continued to be influential in catechisms and manuals for pastoral practice, even in the post-Tridentine period.[67]

Fourth Phase of Development

The Council of Trent played a decisive role in the further development of pastoral and theological understanding. Its declarations on the anointing of the sick are admittedly concerned chiefly with clarifying, against the misinterpretations of the Reformers, the sacramental (and not simply charismatic) status of the rite, its abiding salvific significance for the sick, and the Scriptural character of its manner of administration.

It is nonetheless inescapably clear just what the Coun-

cil intended to decide and what not, and even what conclusions it explicitly wanted drawn from its decisions. It
rejects, above all, the narrow and one-sided Scholastic
doctrine that would allow only the dying to receive the
sacrament. By changing the initially proposed restrictive
words "provided that" to the more open "especially" (expressing what is obviously intended as a pastoral
minimum), the Council laid down an authentic principle
for future thought about the sacrament. Even the fact that
it continues to use the linguistic expressions and spiritual
approaches current in Scholastic teaching and in the pastoral practice of the time (as when, for example, it speaks
of the decisive hour of spiritual struggle) in no way manifests an intention to assign dogmatic value to these (any
more than does the incorporation of St. Thomas' essay *The
Articles of Faith and the Sacraments of the Church* into
the *Decree for the Armenians* at the Council of Florence
[DS 1324-25 (700)]).

The Council's intention was to leave untouched, as far
as possible, the differences of doctrinal opinion within
the Church and to speak in a positive and practical fashion.[69] Consequently, even the canons on the anointing of
the sick contain no specific reference to the anointing as
"sacrament of the dying" nor to the degree of illness required of the recipient; like the early Councils, Trent
speaks simply (three times) of "the sick." The content
(*res*) of the sacrament is said to be the grace of the Holy
Spirit. Its three effects in order of lessening importance
are: eradication of sin and its remnants; supporting and
strengthening of the sick person by awakening trust in
God, by raising his spirits as he carries the burden of
illness, and by strengthening his resistance to demonic
temptation; and, at times ("when it helps to salvation"),
bodily healing as well (DS 1696 [909]).

In opposition, therefore, to Scholastic tendencies toward spiritualism and eschatologism, on the one hand,
and, on the other, to a possible naive, physico-realistic
misunderstanding of the "heavenly medicine" as a sacrament of *bodily* "recovery," Trent opens the way once

again to a renewed, deeper, more integral grasp of the Church's understanding of the anointing of the sick.[70] Despite all that Trent did, however, the necessary correction of existing distortions proceeded only very slowly, and setbacks occurred from time to time.

The post-Tridentine Catechism of Peter Canisius, for example, continues through numerous editions (only two exceptions) to connect "vitality" and "strength" as primary effects (along with the hypothetically admitted alternative of a bodily cure) with the old eschatological commonplace: "that they may depart this life more happily."[71] On the other hand, the language of the Roman Catechism (II, 6) is already less rigid and manifests a broader vision. It usually speaks simply and comprehensively of "the sick" and urges the early administration of the sacrament: "It is obvious that if the Sacrament is administered while consciousness and reason are yet unimpaired, and the mind is capable of eliciting acts of faith and of directing the will to sentiments of piety, a more abundant participation of its graces must be received." Therefore, "though this heavenly medicine is in itself always salutary," pastors should choose the most favorable moment for administering it (II, 6, 9; McHugh and Callan, p. 311). The Catechism also urges greater confidence in regard to the bodily effect along with the spiritual grace (II, 6, 7; 6, 14).

Timely administration of the sacrament continues to be a primary concern in the pastoral synods of the sixteenth and seventeenth centuries.[72] During this period theologians and canonists — with a few exceptions, such as Maldonado and de Coninck[73] — constantly insist on danger of death as a condition for the validity of the sacrament; the distinction between "proximate" and "remote" danger remains purely speculative and verbal. Meanwhile pastoral care of the sick is generally sadly neglected. The largely negative attitude of the synods on the question of repeating the "last anointing" can be understood as a strategy dictated by the desire to accomplish what is practically feasible.[74]

At the end of the seventeenth century, pioneering publications in the history of liturgy, especially the work of the Maurists Mabillon and Martène, were beginning to throw entirely new light on a now languishing practice which had hitherto been regarded as reflecting a unified and apostolic tradition. But there were relatively few independent thinkers in the area of pastoral theology who could emancipate themselves from narrowly doctrinaire conceptions and prepare the way for an understanding derived from biblical and liturgical theology. Among these few was Pope Benedict XIV; in his principal work, *The Diocesan Synod* (1753; VIII, 8,4), he appeals to the "ancient custom of the Church" to justify, for example, a repeated administration of the sacrament. In his letter accompanying the new *Euchologion* for the Uniate Greeks, he no longer speaks of "danger of death," but only of "the sick" or "the seriously sick."[75]

Fifth Phase of Development

In the theological literature of the last two hundred years, the sacrament of the anointing of the sick, often treated simply in a brief appendix to the sacrament of penance,[76] has on the whole been completely dominated by the medieval and thenceforth traditional conception of it as the "sacrament of the dying." Down to Vatican II, with but few exceptions,[77] the high Scholastic thesis about "preparation for glory" is constantly trotted out and refurbished, most recently in existential-eschatological clothing. This conception, though untenable in the light of biblical and liturgical theology, has, especially in the modern period, been widely circulated in the Church through popular literature, very much to the detriment of an authentic understanding of the sacrament in pastoral practice.

For example, since 1937 six editions of Eugen Walter's *The Glory of Christian Death: Holy Anointing as Ultimate Fulfillment of Baptismal Glory* have appealed to Albert the Great, Thomas, Bonaventure, and Duns Scotus as justification for the idea of "the sacramental sealing of death," the last and "crowning anointing" as immediate "preparation of soul and body for perfect glorification," as restoration of baptismal innocence, and as preservation from purgatory. The transfigured atmosphere of the deathbed is here offered as the vital context (*Sitz im Leben*) of the sacrament.[78] It is only a short step to the unhappy term "consecration for death."

More than any other, Michael Schmaus has extensively contributed, through five editions of his widely read *Dogmatics* (1941–57), to spread the thesis (no. 273): "last anointing as consecration for death," and to modernize the Albertine-Thomist conception.[79] The true rediscoverer and defender of this conception must however be considered to be Joseph Kern in his treatise *The Sacrament of Last Anointing* (1907)[80]; he attracted a large following. The phrase "sacrament of consecration for death" itself goes back to Herman Schell, in whose *Dogmatics* (1893) it provides the title for the whole of his rather eccentric discussion of last anointing.[81] It occurs again in L. Winterswyl's *Liturgy for the Laity*,[82] which was quite influential in its day, and finds its way into the literature of theological popularization.[83] The idea was anticipated in Matthias Scheeben's similar but less extreme phrase "consecration for the final struggle" or for the final victory.[84] Scheeben himself does not, however, as is sometimes claimed, speak of a "sacrament of glorification" or of "consecration of the resurrectional body."

This last type of interpretation was reserved for Aloys Grillmeier in our own day. Grillmeier would explain the anointing of the sick as "the sacrament of resurrection" and of "the Christian fulfillment of the whole man."[85] It is clear, however, that his exegesis of James 5:14-15 is misguided by the same doctrinaire presuppositions which dominate modern literature on the sacrament. The very first sentence reads: "Through last anointing . . . the Church admits the dying Christian into eternity" (p. 336). "Death is at the door. The struggle of life is ending" (p. 328). The author is fascinated by "the element of 'ultimacy' from God's point of view" and by "God's final laying hold on man, beyond which there is no other" (p. 334).

The result of Grillmeier's speculations is the most extreme possible eschatological interpretation of the effect of the sacrament on the resurrectional body. Such a view can admittedly appeal to early Scholastic speculation, especially in the school of Abelard (p. 335), but it lacks exegetical foundation.[86] From the viewpoint of biblical theology, the anointing of the sick cannot be regarded as the sacrament of the dying, although this was the meaning assigned to it in the high Middle Ages and is still commonly assigned to it today.[87]

Unfortunately, the theological conclusions deriving from contemporary liturgical science are not sufficiently grasped. Instead, vague pseudo-liturgical arguments from congruity dominate speculation and, even more, the vocabulary of homiletics and catechetics. The supposed analogy with baptism is to be rejected as especially distorting; it makes of the anointing of the sick a "sacrament of initiation" for entry "into the heavenly Church." Such a conception, widespread even among otherwise critical writers, is nothing but a typical doctrinal transmogrification of the old idea of "sacrament of the dying," and is anticipated in early Scholasticism.[88]

6. *Perspectives for Pastoral Theology*

The sacramental theology of the anointing of the sick is still in need of basic dogmatic "clarifications,"[89] and pastoral theology and practice suffer most from the lack. Nothing is gained by an undifferentiated synthesis of Scholastic opinions over the last thousand years or of the "two tendencies in modern theology."[90] Polemical onesidedness, whether in the interests of an eschatological, spiritual "salvation"[91] or of an earthly, bodily "healing,"[92] does even less justice to the basic significance, in liturgical theology, of the anointing of the sick. The liturgy has remained faithful to itself, down to our own day, in its symbolic understanding of the sacrament as "heavenly medicine," and it puts the accent on neither side of this dichotomy. Its basic presupposition is neither "death and danger of death" as a starting-point nor "bodily health and recovery" as a goal.

The sacramental starting-point is *sickness*, and this fact must become firmly established once again in doctrine and in practice. Moreover, sickness here is not a purely medical phenomenon, but when taken in all its dimensions, a situation of salvation or damnation that affects the whole person of the Christian involved.[93] The soteriological realm of sickness is thus the vital context for this sacrament and determines both its symbolism and its inner finality. From this point of view, a certain analogy does exist between it and that other "situational sacrament," penance, with which in the Middle Ages the anointing was unfortunately linked in an unnecessary symbiotic relationship.

In the anointing of the sick the primary concern — the essential one from the viewpoint of sacramental symbolism — is the danger to salvation that arises from sickness as such. This is already to imply an anthropological and soteriological conception of "sickness," and such a conception must become the basis in pastoral theology for a correct and complete understanding of anointing and for its sacramental discipline and pastoral practice. (Modern medicine has taken a decisive turn toward such a comprehensive, psychosomatic-anthropological, person-centered view of illness.) The soteriological concept of illness is also the one which authentically biblico-liturgical texts presuppose, even if at times they may speak directly of "healing" and "restoration of health" instead of speaking, with greater reserve, of "strengthening" and "raising up."[94]

Every serious illness is a critical situation in which salvation or damnation is the issue for the Christian. The latter must prove himself in his life — not just in his death — and in all that it brings: bodily pain; mental depression; isolation from professional life, from human society, from the enjoyment of nature, etc.; impatience and bore-dom; darkness and despair in face of the paradox of suffer-ing; insensitivity and hardening of heart in face of the divine invitation to share in Christ's suffering and, in case of really serious illness, in his Passion and total self-giving to the Father. For such a crisis to exist there need not be the "death agony,"[95] nor need "approaching death" be palpable. Every serious illness is a "decisive situation."[96]

An even wider perspective opens up for us here. Illness as such — as disordering and incipient destruction of human life — is not only subjectively a burdensome trial and a threat to a peaceful "life with God"; it is objectively a disorder in reality itself. As sick men once encountered Christ, the Creator and Redeemer, in his earthly ministry, so now they encounter him in the Church, which sacra-mentally continues his messianic mission and that of the Apostles (cf. Mark 6:7-13; Luke 9:1-6) and gives "his ac-tion spatio-temporal embodiment."[97]

Like the situation of sin, the situation of illness is thus a matter of salvation and a task involving the whole Church. In this critical situation, which most men have to face sooner or later, "the Church, as the primordial sac-ramental embodiment of Christ's salvific presence in the world, becomes active in the way proper to her." That is, she must, in obedience to her mission, carry out the ac-tion Christ willed her to perform in case of illness; that action is the anointing of the sick. The sacrament is therefore not only given as a help to an individual in a particular situation ("a holy sign of entry into illness as into a time of recollection, submission, and trusting self-surrender into the hands of God"[98]); it is also a charac-teristic self-actuation of the Church as instrument of Christ the Redeemer in a universally recurring human situation.

The theology of illness — not just of death — in all its psychological-anthropological and soteriological-mystical dimensions[99] ought to be one of the basic and permanent themes of meditation for the pastoral theologian, and ought to influence all his preaching, guidance of men, and fostering of community. In this perspective, the anointing of the sick is to be viewed as a quite "normal," recurring sacramental form of encounter with Christ, and one which, obviously, is always related both to the measure of the individual's faith and trust and to the unlimited grace which God entrusts to the Church's mediation. There is need that the ecclesiological formula of Leo the Great, "What was manifest in Christ now takes sacramental form in the Church,"[100] should become a formula for dynamic pastoral activity.

The anointing of the sick should not be explained specifically and exclusively as the sacrament of "fufillment," of "glorification," of "sanctification of man's passing," or of "final entry into the Lord's Passion," however noble such conceptions may in themselves be. The anointing of the sick is not "the sacrament of the last illness," even though at times (or, necessarily, even often) it be available for this extreme situation *too*, and though even then it can in its own proper way have a decisive influence for salvation. In brief, judged by what the Bible and the liturgy tell us of the full meaning of anointing the sick, an overstress on the eschatological orientation is a distortion.

Encounter with Christ the Savior, in the days of illness which are critical for salvation, is naught else than the anointing of the sick. When, therefore, the anointing is explained as "the sacrament of consecration of the sick," it is being exaggerated in a way that is unacceptable to sound liturgical theology; it is also being misinterpreted from dogmatic and pastoral-theological viewpoints. "Consecration of the sick" is at best a variant on the "consecration for death" idea and on the medieval discipline which segregated the anointed person from normal life. In the last analysis it leads once again to that fear of the sacrament which the misconception of "last anointing" produced.[101] It is, therefore, inadvisable to speak of "a specific incorporation" of "the anointed . . . into a special ecclesial status,"[102] of "a consecration to a special service of God," or even simply of "a relatively perduring consecration of the sick" which imprints a "quasi-character."[103] The anointing of the sick was instituted as a medicinal, not a consecratory, sign[104]; it is not "the sacrament of consecration" for a supposed ecclesial status of the sick in the Church, but "only" the sacramental means of grace to counteract the "state" of bodily and spiritual weakness which an individual sick person experiences. To put it in broader perspective, it is the ecclesially effected saving encounter of Christ the Redeemer with his brother who is ill and suffering. Every fanciful and theologically forced conception is out of place here. For the same reason, it is inadvisable to put a good deal of emphasis on a connection between anointing of the sick and confirmation, such as some theologians have suggested.[105]

The authentic liturgical, biblical, and patristic tradition knows nothing of all these notions.[106] On the contrary, if we correctly understand the prayers and rites of the anointing of the sick and also keep in mind the "psychology" and "humanness" of this sacrament, we will recognize beyond any doubt that the sacrament, like the Lord himself, answers the burdened sick person's desire for "rescue," "raising up," and "healing." It is these blessings that the Lord brings — though it is healing in a special sense, healing as he understands it and which he alone can make yield salvation: a "healing at the roots" (*sanatio in radice*), we might call it, a "healing of the wounded tap-root."[107]

Amid all this, indeed by very reason of all this, the anointing of the sick, like all the sacraments, retains its deeper relationship to the paschal mystery of the Lord's Passion, death, and resurrection, from which all the sacraments derive their power. But this relationship is not a direct symbolic one in the foreground of the sacrament, as has been claimed at times with an appeal to the anointing at Bethany (Matthew 26:6-13).[109] The anointing of the sick has a more comprehensive and fundamental grace-dimension, which consists in the mastery of those hindrances to salvation which are proper to illness as such.

Taken abstractly, this effect, in the very nature of things, always involves alternatives. Either the inner anointing of the Holy Spirit, which always brings a liberation from sin and some of its effects, also brings the removal of the outward cause which endangers salvation, namely the illness itself, insofar as such a removal is, in God's plan, for the salvation of the sick person; or — and this effect of grace may be expected on every occasion — the interior corporeo-spiritual and personal condition of the sick man is "healed" by a special comprehensive strengthening and restoration of his person in the grace of Christ; that is, he is transformed and made able to achieve his salvation and is liberated from any infection of fatalism. In all this, there must obviously be present with special intensity, as James says, the "prayer of faith" in both the minister and the recipient, and indeed also, and not least, in the community as a whole.[110]

It is therefore only logical that pastoral theology should insist on the anointing of the sick not being deferred to the final stage of illness, as it has unfortunately often been up to now. The anointing is rather to be understood as the sacrament of entry into a conscious state of illness and is to be offered as such by pastors; at the least, it is to be administered at a time when it can exercise its specific sacramental effect fully and without hindrance.[111] Miracles are not a normal effect of the sacraments, and the limited, even "minimum," measure of effectiveness that may be expected from an anointing received only when death is imminent should not be taken as the norm for understanding the sacrament and determining its pastoral value.[112]

If anyone asks what the special "sacrament of homecoming" is, he should, in the earliest and best tradition of the Church, be referred, not to the anointing of the sick, but to the "Last Provision for the Way."[113] The latter is the true sacrament of death, and to it is promised a sharing in Christ's resurrection (John 6:54). Only in cases of necessity, when the reception of Communion is no longer possible, does the anointing of the sick, as far as possible and in its own specific way, replace it in order to offer in the helplessness of the death agony the help which can, of itself, be given to any sick person at any time. Phrases, then, like "the most eschatological of all the sacraments" should be connected not with the anointing of the sick[114] but with holy Viaticum.[115] But here we are already touching on the desiderata in pastoral practice which are suggested by the perspectives we have been discussing.

7. *Desiderata in Pastoral Practice*

The renewal, through liturgical and pastoral theology, of the practice of anointing the sick requires support in three areas: a new overall atmosphere; a discipline renewed from within; and a deeper understanding of the sacramental action.

a) *A New Overall Atmosphere*

In the Western Church,[116] the anointing of the sick is still deprived of a suitable and beneficial climate. A mere change of name has little value. The first need is for the dogmatic theologian to emancipate himself from those a priori conceptions, already mentioned, that arose out of a long-dead discipline, and that have remained permanently dependent on their time and place of origin. These theologians must derive a new orientation from the data of biblical and liturgical theology and from an authentically pastoral-theological grasp of the vital sphere with which the anointing of the sick deals: that is, the sick person in our contemporary, many-sided, anthropological and soteriological understanding of him.

Only by a broader and deeper formation of the clergy in the dogmatic and moral theology of illness can the present unfortunate situation be changed. The priest himself has much to gain here, for he does not like being regarded by the sick as a bringer of "the sacrament of the dying" and as "a forerunner of death."

Such an attempt to renew our understanding of the

anointing of the sick should, evidently, not be misunderstood or misinterpreted as yielding to the contemporary infatuation with the world and its efforts to thrust death as far out of consciousness as possible. Dying with Christ and entering into glory with him must continue to be the great, indispensable, controlling idea of Christian preaching at all times — the more so, in fact, as sickness and death are pushed out of sight in everyday life. But it is one thing to repeatedly open the eyes of the healthy to the "glory of Christian death" (such reminders cannot be too frequent), and another to approach pastoral care of the sick solely from the eschatological viewpoint.

Modern therapy rightly looks to the sacrament of anointing to support the sick person even in the trust he so much needs if he is to be healed and to be master of his situation. In addition, the pastor himself has personal need of a deeper conception, based on biblical and liturgical theology, of the anointing of the sick as a "sacrament of the living," not simply in the technical dogmatic sense, but in the sense of a "sacrament of life" for the specific area of life which being sick is. The interpretation of this area in a pastoral confrontation of biblical revelation with contemporary psychosomatic-anthropological therapy still needs refinement.[117]

Only in these ways will a gradual change of mentality take place in public opinion within the Church. The new atmosphere can be expected to come into being, however, not from repeated exhortations but from the multiplied example of individuals.[118] Only when popes and bishops receive the sacrament at the beginning of their illnesses, and not, as is still the practice even today, "in the face of death," will traditional barriers be broken down and the anointing of the sick become once again "part of a community's everyday life, just as illness is."[119]

The same efforts expended at one time in overcoming other late medieval constraints, e.g., the fear of frequent Communion, will have to be made here as well in order to create a positive "public opinion in the Church" and to turn the anointing of the sick "from a feared to a desired sacrament that brings help to all the sick."[120] Just as formerly when the so-called Easter Communion was imposed, so here we are faced with the same possibility of disciplinary minimism and deferment of the sacrament.

Aversion to the anointing of the sick has, of course, deeper roots than the simple human refusal to think of death. In the last analysis, it indicates a distance from the Church itself and a lack of deeper understanding of the whole sacramental order, of union with Christ, and of vital encounter with Christ in the Church as his primal sacrament. All this is why the anointing of the sick, like the sacraments generally, is understood in such a sadly atomistic and individualistic way.

b) *A New Discipline*

To rescue the anointing of the sick from such misunderstanding, pastoral theology urgently calls for a new approach to the "conditions" and "presuppositions" which, ever since the medieval period of the Western Church, have strait-jacketed the sacrament into a narrowly legal system. The restrictive clauses (the so-called danger of death, the non-repeatability, the exclusion of children) must be loosened and broadened, as in fact they have been to some extent since Trent and especially in recent years.

What is required now of Church authority is reflection of the kind now taken for granted in regard to the Eucharistic fast and to early Communion of children. The restrictions stemming from the rigid Church discipline of the Middle Ages are very difficult to reconcile with the changed medical understanding of the sick person and with the rediscovered original meaning of the sacrament in Bible and liturgy. Even though — or better, precisely because — the so-called danger of death seems today to be under better control due to organized medical diagnosis and prognosis, the psychosomatic burdens of illness (more correctly, of the sick person, since in this area there are always notable differences between individuals) are not only not automatically lightened but perhaps even increased in individual cases. From the soteriological viewpoint, illness continues to be a situation in which salvation or damnation is the issue; as such it is bound up with other factors that cannot be adequately comprehended by the narrow term "danger of death."

Church authority has on numerous occasions made it clear that the "danger of death" condition is not to be overcautiously interpreted,[121] and there has never been an irreversible dogmatic definition that this condition is required for validity.[122] The same is true of the prohibition against repeating the anointing in the same illness, namely, that repetition of the sacrament requires a "new" danger of death after an interval of improvement.[123] In practical pastoral care, such conditions are only hindrances and sources of doubt; they inevitably prove restrictive and, often enough, make the opportune reception of the sacrament very difficult. The question of the point in time at which an illness begins to be a threat to life is secondary, since the sole, ultimately decisive condition is already present: a serious illness that brings spiritual burdens and trials, that is understood by the Christian to put him in a situation critical for his salvation, and that is therefore not only to be converted into a means of personal progress but also to be sacramentally supported and mastered.

More adequate criteria than "danger of death" have already been elaborated for determining whether a vital situation so important for salvation actually exists. Along with old age as such, there are many chronic and long-drawn-out illnesses, such as tuberculosis, paralysis, multiple sclerosis, leukemia, and cancer, which are genuinely and in the fullest sense critical for salvation, and ought therefore to be regarded as sufficient for the sacrament, even if there is no proximate danger of death.[124] Also to be listed here are those illnesses which are rooted in a deep psychosomatic disorder and which, as anthropological medicine is coming to realize better each year, tend to ravage the vital powers unless the sick person receives opportune help at the psychic level.[125] Furthermore, most necessary major surgery is concerned with serious illnesses which are present even before the operation; it is a strange casuistry that would limit the legitimate reception of the sacrament to the hours *after* the operation.

A broad interpretation of the restrictions on repetition of anointing is already permitted.[126] Canon 940, no. 2, which required an interval of "improvement" in the sick person's condition, must now yield to no. 9 of the new *Rite of Anointing*, which provides for repetition of the sacrament during the same illness if the danger becomes more serious.[127]

Finally, seriously sick children, even if not fully capable of sin, should not be refused this sacrament. The usual argument against this practice is the medieval formula for administering the sacrament, which speaks exclusively of the forgiveness of sins.[128] But since the essential meaning of the anointing of the sick does not consist primarily in the forgiveness of sins, as the new rite recognizes, there is no intrinsic reason, to say nothing of the absence of any grounds in biblical and liturgical theology, for excluding children from the encounter with Christ in this sacrament.[129] The early Church and the Christian East practice no exclusion of children.[130] Actually, no. 10 of the new *Rite of Anointing* has settled this problem by specifically allowing sick children to be anointed, provided that they have sufficient use of reason to be comforted by this sacrament.

As far as the dogmatic possibility of a new dispensation in this area and, more generally, of a whole new discipline for the anointing of the sick are concerned, we can say that it is completely within the essential power of the Church over the administration of the sacraments, "provided their substance be safeguarded."[131] The same answer seems adequate for the question of whether a deacon may not in the case of necessity be the extraordinary minister of the sacrament, provided he act thus on the basis of a special hierarchic mission (substituting for a priest) and use oil of the sick that has been consecrated by a bishop or a priest.[132] As far as the consecration of the oil is concerned, the most recent revision of the rite for anointing the sick has, practically speaking, revoked the old decree of the Holy Office (May 15, 1878): "Oil blessed by a priest is completely unsuitable for administering the sacrament of last anointing and cannot be validly used even in extreme necessity."[133] This change is a rather eloquent example of how conscious the Church is, for all her fidelity to the abiding substance of her sacramental tradition, that she has authority from the Lord to responsibly regulate her liturgical and liturgico-pastoral life and to adapt it to changed circumstances.

c) *A New Pastoral Spirituality*

The creation of a new overall atmosphere in the outlook of God's people and a revision of canon law governing the administration of this sacrament are not enough. The most important change of all is that the ministers of the sacrament strive for a radically renewed pastoral spirituality in the area of the anointing of the sick. The anointing should not henceforth be viewed, even in practice, as primarily a simple "provision" (usually reduced to an "essential rite") for the sick. As far, then, as is in his power (for the unforeseen case will occur often enough), the pastor must be careful to prevent situations governed by haste and the pressure of time. Such an attitude will be concerned not only with the greater spiritual profit of the individual sick person but also with the proper liturgical execution of the sacramental celebration itself.

At the beginning of his pastoral activity, every priest still learns from experience how, when administration is reduced to a bare minimum, the sacrament itself is degraded, the minister is in danger of falling into routine, and the whole process threatens to slip into the half-light of magic. In the great hospitals, and especially in the emergency rooms, has not the usual practice of anointing the sick led to inevitable distortion?[134] Has not the "prayer of faith," on which biblical and liturgical tradition lays so much stress, thereby largely languished and disappeared from the consciousness of priests and people?

Especially problematic is the last-minute emergency anointing of dying people or even of people clinically dead (when respiration and circulation have ceased). Admittedly, it is impossible either medically or theologico-anthropologically to determine the exact moment of death, i.e., the definitive dissolution of the person's body-soul unity, which probably varies, in fact, with the vitality of the organism. Admittedly, too, the principle that "extreme cases require extreme measures" is correct in itself.[135] The minister must nonetheless be careful in such cases, especially if the patient is unknown to him, to avoid the scandal of sacramental formalism, to which contemporary man is justifiably quite allergic. He must not, at the urging of a third party or from a desire not to offend sensibilities, let himself be pressured into administering the sacrament as a pious ceremony of "consolation," especially not to unbelievers or to people of other faiths whose intention to receive the sacrament may be positively in doubt.[136]

We need not stress here the fact that the "continuous rite" called for in the Constitution on the Liturgy (no. 74) is concerned only with assuring the proper place of the anointing: *after* confession, if this be required, and *before* Communion. But such a rite could easily be a temptation to "get everything done at once" and would then, especially since the text speaks of "Viaticum," be a new reason for putting the anointing off to the very end. Even independently of confession and Communion, the anointing has its own intrinsic meaning, to the extent that it is received with a penitent and trusting heart, and could even be a spiritual preparation for a later confession, should such be required.

The most urgent requirement for a healthy pastoral spirituality today is that the whole pastoral care of the sick not be reduced to a matter of ritual or, even more exclusively, of sacrament. When rightly understood, the priestly-human visit to the sick can itself, without any liturgical action, become an encounter with Christ and thereby pave the way for the reception of the sacrament, insofar as the pastor brings a bit of the Good News with him and breaks the bread of the Word that comes from God's mouth. Sacraments are to be administered only to believers.

Not only in individual cases but for the community as a whole, the "vital sphere" of sacramental service to the sick must be dismantled and rebuilt from the ground up. Only then can the anointing of the sick, considered until now a sacrament of individual pastoral care, be freed from its isolation and recover that relationship to the ecclesial community which was originally part of it. According to a decree of the Congregation of Rites, March 4, 1965,[137] Ordinaries can allow their priests, despite canon 946, to carry the consecrated oil with them in a suitable container "whenever circumstances make it advisable." This permission need not be seen simply as allowing pastoral provision for the spiritually critical case of "death on the street." It can also mean the revival of an early medieval custom[138] and contribute to greater flexibility in administering the sacrament. The pastor would discover new possibilities in the normal, non-necessary visit to the sick, for in this everyday context he may find "the right moment" or be able to lead the person to it in a natural way. (In such a case he might, as circumstances suggest, dispense with external ritual solemnity to allow all the more room for spontaneous "prayer of faith.") A natural simplicity and a biblical, early Christian directness may perhaps do more than anything else to pull down interior barriers to the sacrament of anointing of the sick.

In any event, however, these informal and individual-oriented approaches to the anointing (James 5:14, "If *one* of you is ill, let *him* call. . . .") should not be one-sidedly stressed. On the contrary, as we have already pointed out, the ecclesial revalorization of the anointing of the sick, that is, its renewed connection with the larger ecclesial community and public (James 5:16, "So confess your sins *to one another*, and pray *for one another*"), has long been a pressing need, and its fulfillment can be decisive for the renewal of the whole pastoral care of the sick.

Once the new rite has created new possibilities for a fully developed communal celebration of the anointing of the sick (by integrating it into the Mass or a Bible service in the church or in the home of the sick person), serious consideration should be given to carrying out the celebration in a meaningful way. The greatly changed social situation of the sick and aged today is favorable to this. In today's hospitals and homes for the elderly, the sick can, for example, get to the chapel with relative ease, in order there to receive the sacrament of anointing and Communion within a communal celebration. In such a more enclosed community, too, many a middle-class prejudice, much timidity in the presence of others, and many a religious misunderstanding could be more easily overcome, and the consolation and power which are the Lord's legacy to us would be experienced in greater peace.

We hope that the hesitations and uncertainty of many pastors will disappear as they learn that even the parish church — for example, on a special day for the sick before or after the major feasts of the year — can become the center of such a sacramental service of the sick, combining the Eucharist and the anointing of the sick into a single liturgical celebration. Should it not be possible for what happens at Lourdes, for example, to happen in every cathedral, in every parish church, and in every home for the elderly as well?[139]

NOTES

[1] Roman Ritual, Title V; Code of Canon Law, canons 937–47; see B. Leurent, "Le Magistère et le mot 'Extrême-Onction' depuis le Concile de Trente," *Analecta Gregoriana*, 68 (1954), 219–32.

[2] Constitution on the Liturgy, no. 73, in Walter M. Abbott (ed.), *The Documents of Vatican II* (New York: America Press, 1966), p. 161.

[3] For a discussion of the final text, see the commentaries, especially E. Lengeling, *Die Konstitution des Zweiten Vatikanischen Konzils über die heilige Liturgie* (Münster, 1964), p. 155; and J. Jungmann, "Commentary on the Constitution on the Liturgy," in H. Vorgrimler (ed.), *Commentary on the Documents of Vatican II*, Vol. 1, tr. by Lalit Adolphus, Kevin Smyth, and Richard Strachan (New York: Herder and Herder, 1967), 53.

[4] Constitution on the Church, no. 11; Decree on the Ministry and Life of Priests, no. 5; Decree on Eastern Catholic Churches, no. 27; the Instruction of September 26, 1964, no. 68, and the preliminary work on the new Ritual (*Notitiae*, 2 [1966], 227). — As late as 1962 the Congregation of Rites expressed opposition to a change of name; see G. Danneels, "La nouvelle Liturgie des Malades dans les diocèses de Belgique," *Paroisse et liturgie*, 44 (1962), 238–53, at p. 245.

[5] For further details, see below, p. 19A.

[6] See F. Cavallera, "Le décret du Concile de Trente sur la Pénitence et l'Extrême-Onction," *Bulletin de littérature ecclésiastique*, 39 (1938), 3–29; B. Botte, "L'onction des malades," *La Maison-Dieu*, no. 15 (1948), 91–107; G. Davanzo, *L'unzione sacra degli infermi* (Turin, 1958), p. 117.

[7] Roman Catechism, Part II, ch. 6, no. 1.

[8] F. Nausea, *Catholicus Catechismus* (Cologne, 1543), fol. 77, ch. 100.

[9] With the appearance of the Catholic Catechism of the German Dioceses (1955), the term "anointing of the sick" gained widespread acceptance.

[10] F. Meurant finds in this "over-restrictive conception" a "threefold error" (theological, liturgical, psychological): see "L'Extême-Onction est-elle le sacrement de la dernière maladie?" *La vie spirituelle*, 92 (1955), 242–51.

[11] See below, notes 79, 81–84, and accompanying text. In a more recent edition, Schmaus entitles his chapter on the anointing of the sick (no. 273) "Anointing of the Sick as Sacrament of Perfection" (*Katholische Dogmatik*, IV/1, 6th ed. [Munich, 1964], 695). We agree

with J. Wiggers that in German the verb *salben* ("to anoint") expresses the symbolic, specifically human action better than does *ölen* ("to oil, lubricate"), which smacks of the mechanic's work; see "'Letzte Ölung' oder 'Krankensalbung,'" *Katechetische Blätter*, 75 (1950), 498–501.

[12] See note 1 above, and Denzinger-Schönmetzer (DS), *Enchiridion Symbolorum* (Freiburg, 1963), nos. 1694–1700 (earlier editions: 907–10) and 1716–19 (926–29). It is significant that once the Code of Canon Law was adopted, certain formulations of the Roman Ritual were altered (e.g., Title V, ch. 1, no. 8). The old text centers chiefly on the pastor's *duty* of anointing the sick ("[the sacrament] should . . . be administered to the sick," or "it ought not be repeated in the same illness"), having in mind, of course, imminent death, which was what those in pastoral care were usually concerned with; the later text speaks rather of the *legitimacy* of administration ("it cannot be administered unless . . .," or "it cannot be repeated unless . . ."); see Botte, *loc. cit.*, p. 104; J.-Ch. Didier, "L'onction des malades et la clause du 'danger de mort,'" *Ami du clergé*, 78 (1968), 97–105.

[13] See note 5 above, and the Constitution on the Liturgy, no. 73.

[14] "Danger of death" as such, without reference to illness or old age, has never been grounds for "last anointing," e.g., before executions, shipwrecks, etc.

[15] Davanzo, *op. cit.*, pp. 105–15; J. Pascher, *Die Liturgie der Sakramente*, 3rd ed. (Münster, 1962); A. Winklhofer, *Kirche in den Sakramenten* (Frankfurt, 1968), p. 197. — In the Decree on Eastern Catholic Churches, no. 27, the Council does not enjoin any stricter supervision on Latin Catholics in a case of intercommunion.

[16] See the new rite; Code of Canon Law, canon 945; Davanzo, *op. cit.*, pp. 53–63. In the Byzantine rite the blessing of the oil at the anointing of the sick is done by the priest himself; the Ambrosian rite allowed the same practice until the end of the eleventh century (see *Libellus de sacramentis* [PL 150:864]) — "a fact overlooked by many dogmatic theologians" (A. Franz, *Die kirchlichen Benediktionen im Mittelater*, 2nd ed. [Freiburg, 1909], J. 343), P. Borella, "L' evoluzione dei riti sacramentali nell' antica liturgia ambrosiana," in W. Durig (ed.), *Liturgie: Gestalt und Vollzug* (Munich, 1963), pp. 48–59.

[17] The fourth canon of Trent is, basically, only rejecting the Reformers' interpretation of the word "presbyter" or "priest."

[18] Davanzo, *op. cit.*, pp. 123–70. — On the conciliar discussion of the first draft of the Constitution on the Liturgy, no. 73, see Jungmann, in Vorgrimler (ed.), *Commentary on the Documents of Vatican II*, p. 53.

19 See Davanzo, *op. cit.*, pp. 69–70. On the question of the scope of earlier limitations on this sacrament, Davanzo's book offers convincing proof that their status is wholly disciplinary, not dogmatic.

20 The liturgy for anointing the sick, as "revised" and newly "prepared" in accordance with the Constitution on the Liturgy (nos. 74–75), lays great stress on this point.

21 Earlier examples of such exhortations (*monitiones*) are provided in A. Dold, *Die Konstanzer Ritualientexte in ihrer Entwicklung von 1482–1721* (Münster, 1923), p. 68, and H. Reifenberg, "Die Ansprache bei der Krankensalbung nach Mainzer Diözesanbrauch seit dem Mittelalter," *Mainzer Zeitschrift*, 60/61 (1965–66), 61–69. — The so-called "Anselmian Questions" (see P. Berger, in *Trierer Theologische Zeitschrift*, 72 [1963], 299–306) have, in themselves, nothing to do with our subject.

22 All the ancient Ambrosian Rituals give to the rite for anointing the sick the title "laying of hands on the sick."

23 The prayer, found as early as the ninth century but unquestionably older than that (see Botte, *loc. cit.*, p. 96), reads as follows: "Lord, our God, through your Apostle James you said: 'If anyone of you is ill, let him summon the elders of the Church and they will pray over him and anoint him with oil in the name of the Lord, and the prayer of faith will bring salvation to the sick person, and the Lord will raise him up again, and if he has sinned, his sins will be forgiven. We pray you, our Redeemer: through the grace of the Holy Spirit cure this man's illness, heal his wounds, and forgive his sins; take away all pain of soul and body, and mercifully grant him full outward and inward health, so that, restored by your mercy, he may be able to perform his [religious] duties as before." See 70B and 77A (see below pages 43, 52) for the current reformulation.

24 Constitution on the Liturgy, no. 75 (Abbott, p. 161). No. 74 speaks somewhat prematurely of "Viaticum."

25 The new rite for the Chrism Mass (1965) brings out these relationships better than the rite of 1956 did; in the latter the readings dealt with the anointing of the sick (James 5:13–16) and the sending of the Apostles to cure the sick (Mark 6:7-13).

26 A collection of the older formulas may be found in E. Bartsch, *Die Sachbeschwörungen der Römischen Liturgie* (Münster, 1967), pp. 404ff.

It will be difficult to apply the commentary here given to the transmogrified official English version given in the United States *Sacramentary* for the Rite of the Blessing of Oils:

Lord God, loving Father,

you bring healing to the sick
through your Son Jesus Christ.
Hear us as we pray to you in faith,
and send the Holy Spirit, man's Helper and Friend,
upon this oil, which nature has provided
to serve the needs of men.
May your blessing ✝
come upon all who are anointed with this oil,
that they may be freed from pain and illness
and made well again in body, mind, and soul.
Father, may this oil be blessed for our use
in the name of our Lord Jesus Christ
(who lives and reigns with you for ever and ever.
℟. Amen.)

[27] C. Ruch and L. Godefroy, "Extrême Onction," *Dictionnaire de théologie catholique*, V/2 (1924), 1966–70 (Ruch); A. Chavasse, "Prières pour les malades et onction sacramentelle," in A.-G. Martimort (ed.), *L'Eglise en Prière: Introduction à la Liturgie* (Tournai 1961) p. 588.

[28] The relative clause in such prayers has varied greatly as to its referent: in Hippolytus, it probably refers to "holiness" (Botte, *La Tradition Apostolique de Saint Hippolyte* [Münster, 1963], pp. 18–19); in the Gelasian Sacramentary, to "blessing" (L. Mohlberg, *Liber Sacramentorum Romanae Aecclesiae ordinis anni circuli* [Cod Vat Reg. lat. 316], [Rome, 1960], p. 61, no. 382); in the Preface for the consecration of chrism in the Roman Pontifical, to "power of the Holy Spirit" and, no less clearly than in the Byzantine consecration of chrism, to the anointing by the Spirit which is prefigured in the "oil of gladness" of Ps. 45:8b (see *Euchologion to mega* [Rome, 1873], pp. 325–26). The reference is correctly interpreted in F. Bourassa, "La grâce sacramentelle de l'Onction des Malades," *Sciences ecclésiastiques*, 19· (1967), 33–47; 20 (1968), 31–58; E. Lanne, "L'onction des martyrs et la bénédiction de l'huile," *Irénikon*, 31 (1958), 152; and in *La Maison-Dieu*, no. 15 (1948), 8; but not, for example, in B. Studer, "Letzte Ölung oder Krankensalbung," *Frieburger Zietschrift für Theologie und Philosophie*, 10 (1963), 45, note 48; J. M. Robert, "Réflexions pour l'intelligence de l'onction des malades," *Présences*, 90 (1965), 97; and S. Zenker, "Das Sakrament der Krankenölung. Seine Theologie und Sein Ritus," *Lebendiges Zeugnis*, 10 (November, 1951), p. 47; etc.

[29] See 1 John 2:20, 27. — For the Christological and pneumatological interpretation of "chrism" (in connection with Ps. 45:8 and the anointing of priests and kings), see also Faustinus, *De trinitate*, 5:2–3 (*PL* 13:71), and Augustine, *Enarrationes in Psalmos*, Ps. 44:19 (*PL*

36:505) and *De civitate Dei*, 20:10 (*PL* 41:676); cf. also *Constitutiones Apostolicae*, 16:3–17:4.

³⁰ Roman Ritual, Title V, ch. 1, no. 1.

³¹ DS 1695 (908): "Anointing aptly symbolizes the grace of the Holy Spirit which invisibly anoints the soul of the sick person."

³² Roman Catechism, II, 6, 5.

³³ For details, see below, notes 84 and 104–5 and the accompanying text.

³⁴ Botte, *loc. cit.*, pp. 94–97; Z. Alszeghy, "L'effetto corporale dell'Estrema Unzione," *Gregorianum*, 38 (1957), 392–96.

³⁵ Roman Catechism, II, 6, 7. [The Roman Catechism is here translated so as to reflect the German writer's interpretation of it. John A. McHugh and Charles J. Callan, *Catechism of the Council of Trent for Parish Priests*, 2nd ed. (New York: Wagner, 1934), p. 310, translate the Latin "*Nullum enim est aliud Sacramentum, quod pluribus precibus conficiatur*" as "There is no Sacrament, the administration of which is accompanied by more numerous prayers."]

³⁶ See F. Mussner, *Der Jakobusbrief* (Freiburg, 1964), pp. 218–25.

³⁷ Origen, *In Leviticum homiliae*, 2:4 (*PG* 12:419).

³⁸ See Matthew 10:1; Mark 6:12, 16:18. Also J. Hempel, *Heilung als Symbol und Wirklichkeit im biblischen Schrifttum*, 2nd ed. (Göttingen, 1965), p. 291.

³⁹ It is not clear from the subordinate conditional clause in James 5:15c whether a general state of sin is meant (Vulgate: "if he be in sin[s]") or a sin committed because of the person's state of illness (Greek: "if he have committed any sins").

⁴⁰ There can be no legitimate a priori appeal to the medieval Scholastic (and, later, popular) conception of "the sacrament of the dying"; see below, note 85.

⁴¹ R. Svoboda, "Das Sakrament der Krankenölung," *Theologisch-praktische Quartalschrift*, 96 (1948), 295–303, at p. 297; F. Schreibmayr and K. Tilmann (eds.), *Handbuch zum Katholischen Katechismus*, II/2 (Freiburg, 1966), 603.

⁴² A. d'Alès, "Extrême-Onction," *Dictionnaire de la Bible: Supplément* III (Paris, 1938), 265; cf. H. Spaemann, "Das Sakrament der Krankensalbung," *Liturgie und Mönchtum*, 25 (1959), 31–32.

⁴³ This is the point made in canon 1 of the Council of Trent (DS 1716 [926]); see K. Rahner, *The Church and the Sacraments*, tr. by W. J. O'Hara (New York: Herder and Herder, 1963), p. 61, note 4.

⁴⁴ B. Poschmann, *Penance and the Anointing of the Sick*, tr. and

rev. by Francis Courtney, S.J. (New York: Herder and Herder, 1964), p. 236. — The recent exciting report of the discovery of a piece of silver foil dating from the first century and containing prayers in Judaeo-Aramaic for the anointing of the sick (cf. E. Testa, *L'Huile de la foi: L'onction des malades sur une lamelle du premier siècle* [Jerusalem, 1967] proved erroneous; the find was, instead, an early medieval, non-Christian magical text (cf. J. C. Milik, "Une amulette Judéo-araméenne," *Biblica*, 48 [1967], 450–51).

[45] Venerable Bede, *Commentary on the Letter of James:* "Not priests alone, but all Christians, as Pope Innocent writes, may use this oil for anointing in their own or others' need; but only the bishop may consecrate the oil. 'Oil in the name of the Lord' means oil consecrated in the name of the Lord" (*PL* 93:39).

[46] A. Chavasse, *Étude sur l'onction des infirmes dans l'Église Latine du IIIe au XIe siècle*, I: *Du IIIe siècle à la Réforme Carolingienne* (Lyons, 1942), pp. 117ff.; H. Rondet, "Extrême-Onction," *Dictionnaire de spiritualité*, 4 (Paris, 1960), col. 2192.

[47] Botte, *loc. cit.*, pp. 92–93.

[48] Especially impressive examples are the prayer for the consecration of oil in Serapion (Rouet de Journel, *Enchiridion patristicum*, no. 1241) and a prayer from the early Spanish *Liber ordinum* (ed. M. Férotin [Paris, 1904]), quoted in Alszeghy, *loc. cit.*, p. 399

[49] Chavasse, "Prières . . ." (note 27 above), p. 588.

[50] Innocent I, *Letter* 25:8 (Denzinger-Schönmetzer, 216 [99]); cf. Rondet, *loc. cit.*, cols. 2192–93.

[51] See above, note 45.

[52] Bede refers to James 5:14-15 in the same breath with Mark 6:12 and concludes: "It is evident, then, that the Apostles themselves established the ecclesiastical custom of anointing the *energumeni* [sick persons whose illness was attributed to demonic influence] and any other sick person with oil blessed by a bishop"(*CCL* 120:506, cf. 196). Bede's words are constantly cited in later times; cf. J.-Ch. Didier and H. R. Philippeau, "Extrême-Onction," *Catholicisme*, 4 (Paris, 1956), col. 2194.

[53] See J. Jungmann, *Die lateinischen Bussriten in ihrer geschichtlichen Entwicklung* (Innsbruck, 1932), pp. 114–15.

[54] Didier-Philippeau, *loc. cit.*, cols. 995ff., 1007, Chavasse, *Étude . . .*, pp. 13–21, and "Prières . . .," pp. 586, 588–89. See especially the *Capitulary* of Theodulf of Orleans (*PL* 105:220ff.).

[55] C. de Clercq, "Ordines unctionis infirmi des IXe et Xe siècles," *Ephemerides Liturgicae*, 44 (1930), 100–32; Botte, *loc. cit.*, pp. 93ff.

[56] Didier-Philippeau, *loc. cit.*, col. 1009, offer as an example a "Ritual" of the tenth century (monastery of Lerins?). It begins: "Rite for visiting and anointing the sick person and for bringing him holy Communion, as well as for his death and burial," and ends: "End of the rite for the sick or dying."

[57] See above, note 12, for an analogous transition from the one approach to the other.

[58] See P. Browe, "Die Letzte Ölung in den abendländischen Kirchen des Mittelalters," *Zeitschrift für katholische Theologie*, 55 (1931), 526ff., 558ff. According to the Madrid Treatise *De septem sacramentis*, the recipient of the sacrament, "if he recover from his illness, may not return to his earlier style of life, since, once anointed, he is dead to this world." Consequently a married man could not receive the last anointing "without his wife's permission." See H. Weisweiler, "Das Sakrament der Letzten Ölung in den systematischen Werken der ersten Frühscholastik," *Scholastik*, 7 (1932), 546, note 71.

[59] See Ivo of Chartres, *Letter* 255: "I do not think that the anointing should be repeated, for, in the view of the Apostolic See, such is the nature of this sacrament. . . . For the anointing of the sick is a rite of public penance which may not be repeated any more than baptism may, as Augustine and Anselm testify" (*PL* 162:260).

[60] According to Magister Simon, this anointing consecrates all a man's senses to God: "It seems the better view that the sacrament should not be repeated and that the person who has consecrated all his senses to God by this anointing should be unwilling to soil them again by any tainted earthly occupation" (Weisweiler, *loc. cit.*, p. 546, note 71). Voices were indeed raised against such a "lay opinion" or "foolish opinion" (Weisweiler, *loc. cit.*, note 75); for example, the English bishop Aelfric (*ca.* 1005) disputed the view of "some" that the sacrament involved "a consecration [*ordinatio*]" (Browe, *loc. cit.*, pp. 558–59). But the very question asked in a twelfth-century Roman Pontifical: "If the Lord shows you mercy and heals you, will you preserve it [the anointing]?" (M. Andrieu, *Le Pontifical Romain du Moyen-Age*, 1 [Vatican City, 1938], 267), reflects the idea of a "consecration" (see Botte, *loc. cit.*, p. 96). Thomas Aquinas rejects the idea of a "consecration" in *Summa theol., Suppl.*, q. 30, a. 3, ad 2; see below, note 103.

[61] Typical is the revision of a Magdalene College pontifical (twelfth century) in which the concluding prayer ("God, who through your Apostle . . .") replaces the original (pre-ninth-century) clause "that through your mercy he be restored to his duties" with the entirely new clause "that he may obtain the forgiveness of his sins and come to eternal life" (see Botte, *loc. cit.*, p. 96).

[62] Such contact with the East was still possible at the end of the eighth century, as is shown by the *Capitulary* of Theodulf of Orleans; see Didier-Philippeau, *loc. cit.*, col. 1001.

[63] See, e.g., Magister Simon's analogy with baptism: "As baptism is the sacrament of those entering, so this anointing is the sacrament of those departing. Baptism signs men with the mark of Christ as they enter the world; anointing brings the departing to the vision of God" (Weisweiler, *loc. cit.*, p. 345, note 95).

[64] Saint Thomas d'Aquin, *Somme théologique: L'Extrême-Onction (Suppl. 9, 29–33)*, translation, notes, and appendices by H.-D. Gardeil (Paris, 1967), p. 116.

[65] On Scotus' analysis of the agony, which, with its anxiety and pain, makes genuine repentance impossible, see Alszeghy, *loc. cit.*, p. 402.

[66] Poschmann, *op. cit.*, p. 247.

[67] See below, note 71. In the "Examination for Ordinands" composed by F. J. Ferus, Franciscan Guardian and cathedral preacher, we read: "The effect of this anointing is to confer the grace of the Holy Spirit for purification from venial sin, and its aim is a happy and safe death in the Lord" (quoted in F. Nausea, *Catholicus Catechismus* [Antwerp, 1551], p. 302).

[68] Cavallera, *loc. cit.*, p. 25; Botte, *loc. cit.*, p. 100.

[69] See *Concilium Tridentinum* (Görresgesellschaft), *Acta*, III, pp. 311–17, 329, 358–59; see Davanzo, *op. cit.*, pp. 85ff.

[70] We need not accept Poschmann's view that Trent "by the sanction which it gave in general to the doctrines worked out by the Scholastics . . . brought the development of the dogmatic teaching on the anointing of the sick to a close for the time being" (*op. cit.*, p. 257).

[71] Streicher's edition of Canisius' Catechisms, I, pp. 253–54, 320; II, pp. 63–64. Exceptions: I, p. 269; II, p. 150.

[72] Davanzo, *op. cit.*, pp. 91, 95.

[73] Davanzo, *op. cit.*, pp. 92ff.

[74] Davanzo, *op. cit.*, p. 142, note 6.

[75] *Monitum* III of *Letter* 1, "Ex quo primum" (March 1, 1756), reads: "In addition, priests ought to bear in mind that the sacrament of holy oil or Euchelaion was instituted by Christ as heavenly medicine not for the soul's salvation alone, but for the body's health as well, and therefore is to be administered only to the sick, not to those in good health, and at a time when they are conscious and aware of what they are doing" (no. 44). In the subsequent clarification of this *Monitum* (no. 46), the Pope speaks of "the gravely ill" but at the same time, appealing

to Mabillon and Martène, approves of cases in which the sick can still make their way to church on foot in order there to receive the anointing (*Bullarium*, IV [Rome, 1762], pp. 167–68).

[76] Botte, *loc. cit.*, p. 91: "like a poor cousin."

[77] For example, H. Baumeister, *Lexikon für Theologie und Kirche*, 7 (1935), 716; R. Svoboda, *loc. cit.*, p. 299.

[78] E. Walter, *Die Herrlichkeit des christlichen Sterbens: Die heilige Ölung als letzte Vollendung der Taufherrlichkeit* (1937ff.). In 1965 a new title was used: *The Twofold Birth: Beginning and Fulfillment of Christian Existence*. In his book *Selig, die im Herrn sterben* (Mainz, 1962), Walter presents this view in somewhat more moderate fashion, but even here he appeals to the eschatological conception developed in high Scholasticism (pp. 97–101).

[79] See note 11, above. In the most recent edition Schmaus substitutes "Sacrament of Fulfillment" for "Consecration for Death," but the substance remains unchanged (no. 714).

[80] J. Kern, *De sacramento extremae unctionis*, p. 81; "Proposition 5. The purpose of last anointing is the soul's perfect health and immediate entry into glory, unless the restoration of bodily health to naturally mortal man be more expedient for him." Even the collection of documents *The Teaching of the Catholic Church as Contained in Her Documents*, ed. by Josef Neuner, S.J., Heinrich Roos, S.J., and Karl Rahner, S.J.; tr. by Geoffrey Stevens (Staten Island, N.Y.: Alba House, 1967) entirely approves of the idea that "man . . . stands at the threshold of eternity . . . ready to enter directly upon the Beatific Vision" (p. 331).

[81] Herman Schell, *Katholische Dogmatik*, III/2 (Paderborn, 1893), p. 614. For Schell, last anointing is presumed to be the sacrament of the death agony or, as he puts it, of "the restricted personality" which "in the inevitable dissolution of nature is more or less wholly or partially restricted and hindered in the exercise of moral choice," so that the sacrament of penance becomes difficult or impossible (pp. 615, 631–32). At bottom, this is Duns Scotus' view.

[82] L. Winterswyl, *Laienliturgik*, 2 (2nd ed.; Kevelaer, 1938), pp. 148–54.

[83] See, for example, R. Graber, *Christus in seinen heiligen Sakramenten* (2nd ed.; Munich, 1940), especially pp. 132–43; E. Biser, *Christusgeheimnis der Sakramente* (Heidelberg, 1950), pp. 22, 91.

[84] M. Scheeben, *The Mysteries of Christianity*, tr. by Cyril Vollert, S.J. (St. Louis: B. Herder, 1946), pp. 577–78.

[85] A. Grillmeier, "Das Sakrament der Auferstehung: Versuch einer

Sinndeutung der Letzten Ölung," *Geist und Leben*, 34 (1961), 326–36.

[86] See Mussner, *op. cit.*, p. 223.

[87] Unfortunately, Grillmeier introduces his ideas on the sacrament into his commentary on the Constitution on the Liturgy, no. 11, in Vorgrimler (ed.), *Commentary on the Documents of Vatican II*, Vol. 1, p. 163.

[88] Graber speaks of a "baptism with oil" (*op. cit.*, pp. 132–33); Rondet: "a sacrament of initiation, as it were, into eternal life" (*loc. cit.*, col. 2198); Grillmeier: "Baptism is the sacrament of initiation, and anointing the visible sign of dismissal from the visible community of the Church in this world" (*loc. cit.*, p. 336), M.-M Philippon: "As baptism is the sacrament of initiation into the divine life, so extreme unction marks the departure from this life to the Father's house in heaven" (*The Sacraments in Christian Life*, tr. by John A. Otto [Westminster, Md., 1954], p. 354). A classical example of now standard catechetical and homiletic language can be found in Michael Faulhaber's Pastoral Letter of 1912: "Baptism is the Savior's morning blessing at the first hour of life, last anointing his evening blessing at the eleventh hour. Confirmation anoints man for the battle of life, last anointing for the battle of death" (*Zeitfragen und Zeitaufgaben* [Freiburg, 1923], p. 35). See above, note 63.

[89] Rondet, *loc. cit.*, col. 2197.

[90] Studer, *loc. cit.*, p. 33.

[91] See Grillmeier, *loc. cit.*

[92] See J.-Ch. Didier, *Death and the Christian*, tr. by P. J. Hepburne-Scott. Twentieth-Century Encyclopedia of Catholicism, 55 (New York: Hawthorn, 1961), pp. 53–59.

[93] Meurant, *loc. cit.*, pp. 244–45.

[94] See above, notes 34, 47–48.

[95] Rahner, *The Church and the Sacraments*, p. 67.

[96] Rahner, *Bergend und heilend* (Munich, 1965), pp. 5ff.

[97] Rahner, *The Church and the Sacraments*, p. 39.

[98] See Rondet, *loc. cit.*, col. 2198.

[99] On this point, see L. M. Weber, "Krankheit," *Lexikon für Theologie und Kirche*, 6 (Freiburg, 1961), cols. 591–95; Herbert Vorgrimler, "Lebensphasen," *Lexikon für Theologie und Kirche*, 6, col. 865. Long ago, Rabanus Maurus saw in James 5:14 a reference to a means of grace to counteract the despair and hopelessness which illness engenders (*Commentary on Ecclesiastes*, 8:14 [*PL* 109:1032]).

[100] Leo the Great, *Sermon* 74:2, (*PL* 54:348).

[101] See Bonaventure, *In IV Sent*, d. 23, a. 1, q. 2: "a person is anointed . . . as a king that he may enter the kingdom of heaven as his own."

[102] E. Schillebeeckx, O.P., *Christ the Sacrament of the Encounter with God* (New York: Sheed & Ward, 1963), p. 176.

[103] Studer, *loc. cit.*, pp. 42–46, 53–54. See St. Thomas, *Summa theol.*, *Suppl.*, q. 30, a. 3: "This sacrament is simply a remedy and does not depute a person to do or receive anything."

[104] A.-G. Martimort, *The Signs of the New Covenant* (Collegeville, Minn., 1963), p. 264; and St. Thomas, *Summa theol.*, *Suppl.*, q. 30, a. 3, ad 2: "The anointing in ordination and confirmation is consecratory and deputes a person for a sacred task; the anointing here is medicinal."

[105] Winklhofer, *op. cit.*, pp. 194, 202; Zenker, *loc. cit.*, *passim*.

[106] See especially Alszeghy, *loc. cit.*

[107] J. Betz, "Krankensalbung," in H. Fries (ed.), *Wort und Sakrament* (Munich, 1966), pp. 199–208.

[108] Constitution on the Liturgy, no. 61 (Abbott, p. 158).

[109] Studer, *loc. cit.*, pp. 45–46.

[110] Roman Catechism, II, 6, 7 (see above, note 35 and corresponding text).

[111] Roman Catechism, II, 6, 9.

[112] Therefore, too, the "spiritual transformation" of the sick person so that he "dies in peace" — a phenomenon witnessed at times by priests ministering to the sick — should not be unduly stressed; see "Pratique de l'onction des malades: Deux enquêtes," *Présences*, 90 (1965), 45–74.

[113] The term "Viaticum" has undergone a change of meaning like that of the anointing of the sick. The Council of Nicea expresses itself very carefully when it speaks of the "*last* and most necessary Ephodion [provision for the traveler]" (Mansi, 2:673). Down to the high Middle Ages, "viaticum" with a qualifier meant simply Communion (see A. Bride, "Viatique," *Dictionnaire de théologie catholique*, XV/2 (1950), 2843). The Roman Catechism was still familiar with this unrestricted use.

[114] As Studer, *loc. cit.*, p. 119, connects it.

[115] See the lively essay of L. Beauduin, "Le Viatique," *La Maison-Dieu*, no. 15 (1948), 116–29.

[116] For the Eastern Churches, see Didier-Philippeau, *loc. cit.*, cols. 1002–3; recent currents in Protestantism, Anglicanism, and Orthodoxy are reported in *Présences*, 90 (1965), 113–42.

[117] Robert, *loc. cit.*, 91–100; and note 99 above.

[118] Robert, *loc. cit.*, p. 93, note 1, tells of a "James League" founded by Canon Barba of Nice, whose members bind themselves "on every occasion to oppose the erroneous view that the anointing of the sick is simply a help in the death struggle."

[119] Winklhofer, *op. cit.*, p. 202.

[120] Winklhofer, *op. cit.*, p. 201.

[121] See Pius XI, *Acta Apostolicae Sedis*, 13 (1923), 342.

[122] Davanzo, *op. cit.*, p. 113.

[123] Code of Canon Law, canon 940, no. 2.

[124] On this point, see "Pratique de l'onction des malades: Deux enquêtes," *Présences*, 90 (1965), 65ff., 70–71; Winklhofer, *op. cit.*, p. 197. A decree of the Congregation for the Propagation of the Faith, February 20, 1801, expressly allowed an early administration of the sacrament when the priest might not be easily reached for long periods.

[125] Spaemann, *loc. cit.*, p. 33, rightly asks whether severe neurotics, people with mental disorders, and similar patients who are "not in any recognizable danger of death" but the "Christian character of whose death is clearly endangered" do not have a right to be anointed. A reference to the early Church's practice of anointing *energumeni* is pertinent here; see above, note 52.

[126] Davanzo, *op. cit.*, pp. 169–70.

[127] Kern, *op. cit.*, pp. 338ff., as long ago as 1907 offered strong arguments in defense of the possibility of frequent repetition.

[128] Thus St. Thomas, *Summa theol.*, *Suppl.*, q. 32, a. 4 (see Gardeil, *op.cit.*, pp. 76ff.). Here again, in the last analysis, a minimum required in pastoral practice became a doctrinal principle. Insistence that the sacrament must be administered to children over fourteen led to the conclusion that it may not be administered to children under fourteen (even, at times, under eighteen); see M. Andrieu, "Le Viatique et l'Extrême-Onction des enfants," *Revue pratique d'apologétique* (1912), 93ff., 95, 97–98; Ruch-Godefroy, *loc. cit.*, cols. 1996–97.

[129] In agreement are Svoboda, *loc. cit.*, p. 300, and M. Capello, *De extrema unctione* (Turin, 1942), p. 154.

[130] Theodulf of Orleans recommends the anointing of sick children; see Didier-Philippeau, *loc. cit.*, col. 1010.

[131] Council of Trent, Sess. 21, ch. 2 (DS 1728 [931]).

[132] See above, note 17. This desideratum has recently been expressed once again in various quarters: e: g., J.-Ch. Didier, "Sur le min-

istère de l'Onction des Malades," *Ami du clerge*, 74 (1964), 488–93, cited by Robert, *loc. cit.*, p. 105; M. Coune, "L'onction des malades." *Paroisse et liturgie*, 49 (1967), 586. For earlier defenders of this position, see Weisweiler, *loc. cit.*, pp. 535–42.

[133] See Ruch-Godefroy, *loc. cit.*, col. 2014, and DS 2762–63 (1628–29).

[134] See "Pratique de l'onction des malades: Deux enquêtes," *op. cit.*, pp. 49–54.

[135] J. Policha, "Die Krankensalbung," in R. Svoboda (ed.), *Berufsethik der Katholischen Krankenpflege* (Kevelaer, 1967), pp. 164–65.

[136] J. Robilliard, "Das Sakrament der Krankensalbung," *Die Katholische Glaubenswelt*, 3 (Freiburg, 1961), 599; Robert, *loc. cit.*, p. 110; "Pratique de l'onction des malades: Deux enquêtes," *op. cit.*, pp. 53ff.

[137] Published in *Osservatore Romano*, March 19, 1965.

[138] According to the so-called *Statutes of Boniface*, priests are always to carry the holy oils on their person (Mansi, 12:384v, 386).

[139] Among the position papers for the Diocesan Synod of Vienna, 1969, there is a "Proposal for Public Administration of the Anointing of the Sick"; see E. Höfling, in *Bibel und Liturgie*, 41 (1968), 251.

STUDY AID QUESTIONNAIRE

NAME AND INTERPRETATION *pages* 5A–6A

Historical emphases frequently are manifested in names and key words. How does this apply to the sacrament under consideration? State in precise terms the position of the Council of Trent on Anointing as the "sacrament of the dying." Cite several instances in which the imprecise name "Last Anointing" precipitated novel and untraditional interpretations of this sacrament.

CANONICAL PRESCRIPTIONS — *pages* 6A–9A

Discuss several distinct ways in which the phrase "danger of death" may be understood; relate these possibilities to the usage of the phrase in (a) Canon Law; (b) the Constitution on the Sacred Liturgy; (c) Scholastic theology; (d) current popular idiom. How would you list the predispositions for a spiritually fruitful reception of the sacrament of Anointing?

Specifically, how would familiarity with the liturgy of Holy Thursday as given in the sacramentary add to an appreciation of this sacrament? It is proper procedure for a priest to bless the oil for use at Anointing with little regard to the availability of oil consecrated by the bishop on Holy Thursday? What does the rite itself say concerning the minister of Anointing? Distinguish between the solemn form of the sacrament and its administration in case of necessity; discuss the "continuous rite" as given in the ritual itself.

THE LITURGY OF THE SACRAMENT — *pages* 9A–12A

What is the content of Nos. 61–63 in the Constitution on the Sacred Liturgy? Outline in detail the administration of the sacrament of Anointing from the rite as given on pages 40–59 in this book. Analyze the nucleus of the sacramental administration and develop at least six topics that could well serve as themes for a homily or a catechetical lesson.

Discuss the liturgy for the consecration of the oil as done by a bishop on Holy Thursday. What are some of the spiritual-theological themes to which expression is given? How does the symbolism inherent in the use of oil help define correctly the nature and purpose of its supernatural use? The Roman Catechism insisted that Anointing is the only sacrament to be "brought into existence by numerous prayers"; explain.

SCRIPTURAL SOURCE — *pages* 13A–15A

Read all of chapter five in the Letter of St. James; consult a commentary on the whole chapter. How does this full setting aid in an understanding of verses 14-16? Does the interpretation given in your commentary harmonize with that on pages 13A–14A? How would you summarize the spiritual message contained in the verses under consideration?

HISTORICAL DEVELOPMENT OF PASTORAL PRACTICE — *pages* 15A–16A

Why is the distinction between the biblical and liturgical aspects of Anointing and its historically conditioned forms of particular importance in the pastoral application of this sacrament? How many distinct phases of historical development does our author propose for consideration? Indicate the specific characteristics of each of these five phases.

FIRST PHASE OF DEVELOPMENT — *pages* 16A–17A

What was Christian thinking and practice on the Anointing of the sick before the time of Venerable Bede in the seventh century? What importance was given to the solemn blessing of the oil by the bishop? Who could be the "ministers" of the sacrament? How would you detail the relationship between physical and spiritual values related to anointing in the religious thought of that early period? State several ways in which emphases regarding the methods of administration and the purposes of the sacrament were modified about the eighth century A.D.

SECOND PHASE OF DEVELOPMENT — *pages* 17A–19A

Where and when did rituals and pastoral instructions for the care of the sick make their first appearance? How were priests and penitential practices related to this new approach? Was it a reasonable and easy association that led to relating the sacrament of Anointing to persons mortally ill or dying? The phrase "unhealthy spiritualism" is used by our author; explain.

THIRD PHASE OF DEVELOPMENT — *pages* 19A–22A

Tell something about the saints who were the great masters of high Scholasticism. If these great saints and doctors of the Church were the creators of "the new and flourishing theology of the sacraments," how is it that their contributions are so little esteemed? Does it seem likely that these doctors of the Church regarded physical healing as an "infallible" effect of the sacrament of Anointing? Our author states: "The spirituality of the age . . . was shaped by the idea of preparing for eternity." Was that really so deplorable?

"The fundamental text on which all Scholastic reflection is based and to which it refers as a norm" is taken from Peter Lombard. Would St. Thomas and St. Albert the Great accept this evaluation of their work or would they say that the Bible, the Fathers of the Church and Catholic piety had been "fundamental"?

FOURTH PHASE OF DEVELOPMENT — *pages* 22A–25A

What role did the Council of Trent perform in the area of clarifying pastoral and theological problems concerning the sacrament of Anointing? In what specific way did the Council of Trent open new ways of understanding the purpose and efficacy of this sacrament?

The Roman Catechism or the Catechism of the Council of Trent has a number of important directives regarding the sacrament of the sick; explain some of these. How do personages such as Mabillon and Martene enter the picture? And what was the position of Pope Benedict XIV?

FIFTH PHASE OF DEVELOPMENT — *pages* 25A–27A

Discuss what is meant by the Scholastic thesis "preparation for glory" and the "unhappy term: consecration for death." How would you evaluate the position of Aloys Grillmeier? Give solid evidence that pastoral practice and Catholic piety accented the worst in these various explanations and consequently derived little or no benefit from the sacrament of holy Anointing for many centuries.

PERSPECTIVES FOR PASTORAL THEOLOGY — *pages* 27A–33A

In the anointing of the sick the primary concern . . . is the danger to salvation that arises from sickness as such; enlarge upon this statement.

Our understanding of sickness must be open to ever widening perspectives; what are some of the implications of this position?

Like the situation of sin, the situation of illness is a matter of salvation and a task involving the whole Church; discuss the ramifications of this assertion. Give an outline of a "theology of sickness." How is this sacrament related to the paschal mystery of the Lord's Passion, death, and resurrection, from which all the sacraments derive their power?

The "Last Provision for the Way" is the true sacrament of death, and to it is promised a sharing in Christ's resurrection; give further comment.

DESIDERATA IN PASTORAL PRACTICE — *pages* 33A–41A

Cite the three areas that would contribute immensely to a more fruitful understanding and use of the sacrament of the sick. How would the first of these, namely, a new overall atmosphere, aid the cause? What would be some down-to-earth popular practices that would help in rehabilitating this sacrament?

Along with old age as such, there are many chronic and long-drawn-out illnesses, such as tuberculosis, paralysis, multiple sclerosis, leukemia, and cancer, which are genuinely and in the fullest sense critical for salvation;

relate these conditions to the new discipline that needs to become part of Church practice.

Seriously sick children, even if not fully capable of sin, should not be refused this sacrament; what does the official text of the Rite of Anointing have to say on this point?

Discuss what is meant by "a new pastoral spirituality" with regard to the Anointing of the sick. What are the advantages and the disadvantages associated with the "continuous rite" of the sacraments for the sick? How does the Church's official ritual provide against reducing the care of the sick to a bare minimum? List a number of ways by which you would supplement the general directives given in the ritual with specific plans or programs.

Suggested Supplementary Reading

The Sacrament of Anointing the Sick by Monsignor Charles J. Keating; pages 8–17 in *Homiletic and Pastoral Review*, June 1974.

Study Text II — Anointing and Pastoral Care of the Sick edited by the Bishops' Committee on the Liturgy; available from: Publications Office, United States Catholic Conference, 1312 Massachusetts Avenue, N.W., Washington, D.C. 20005.

Background Catechesis: Rite for the Anointing and Pastoral Care of the Sick available from: Federation of Diocesan Liturgical Commissions, Route 1 Box 39, Pevely, Missouri 63070.

Christian Healing, New Catholic Encyclopedia, vol. 6, pages 960–962.

Sacraments of Healing and of Vocation by P. F. Palmer. Prentice Hall, Englewood Cliffs, New Jersey.

The Mystery of Suffering and Death edited by Michael J. Taylor; Alba House, Staten Island, New York.

The New Rite of Anointing by T. E. Tierney; pages 30–37 in *Pastoral Life*, vol. 22 (1973).

The New Rite for the Sacrament of the Sick by Martin Slattery; pages 131–137 in *The Furrow*, vol. 24 (1973).

The Signs of the New Covenant by Aimé Georges Martimort. The Liturgical Press, Collegeville, Minn. 56321.

RITE OF ANOINTING

and

PASTORAL CARE OF THE SICK

Provisional Text

THE ROMAN RITUAL

revised by decree of the Second Vatican
Ecumenical Council
and published by authority of Pope Paul VI

RITE OF ANOINTING

and

PASTORAL CARE OF THE SICK

Provisional Text

Prepared by the International Committee on English
in the Liturgy

Approved for Interim use in the Dioceses of the United States
of America by the Bishops' Committee on the Liturgy and the
Executive Committee of the National Conference of Catholic
Bishops and Confirmed by the Apostolic See

1974

THE LITURGICAL PRESS

Collegeville   **Minnesota**

Concordat cum originali: † George H. Speltz, Bishop of St. Cloud, Minnesota. January 21, 1974.

English translation of the Rite of Anointing and Pastoral Care of the Sick copyright © 1973, International Committee on English in the Liturgy, Inc. All rights reserved.

The text of the Revised Standard Version — Catholic Edition of the Holy Bible contained in this book is used by permission, copyright © 1965 and 1966 by the Division of Christian Education of the National Council of Churches of Christ in the United States of America. All rights reserved.

Published by authority of the Bishops' Committee on the Liturgy, National Conference of Catholic Bishops.

Copyright © 1974, The Order of St. Benedict, Inc., Collegeville, Minnesota. Printed in U.S.A.

CONTENTS

SACRED CONGREGATION
FOR DIVINE WORSHIP

Prot. no. 1501/72

DECREE

When the Church cares for the sick, it serves Christ himself in the suffering members of his Mystical Body. When it follows the example of the Lord Jesus, who "went about doing good and healing" (Acts 10:38), the Church obeys his command to cure the sick (see Mark 16:18).

The Church shows this solicitude not only by visiting those who are in poor health but also by raising them up through the sacrament of anointing and by nourishing them with the eucharist during their illness and in danger of death. Finally, the Church offers prayers for the sick to commend them to God, especially in the last moments of life.

To make the meaning of anointing clearer and more evident, the Second Vatican Council decreed: "The number of the anointings is to be adapted to the occasion, and the prayers which belong to the rite of anointing are to be revised so as to correspond with the varying conditions of the sick who receive the sacrament." [1] The council also directed that a continuous rite be prepared according to which the sick man is anointed after he has made his confession and before he receives viaticum. [2]

In the apostolic constitution **Sacram Unctionem infirmorum** of November 30, 1972, Pope Paul VI established a new sacramental form of anointing and approved the **Rite of Anointing and Pastoral Care of the Sick.** The Congregation for Divine Worship prepared this rite and now issues it, declaring this to be the typical edition so that it may replace the pertinent titles which are now in the Roman Ritual.

Anything to the contrary notwithstanding.

From the office of the Congregation for Divine Worship, December 7, 1972.

> **Arturo Card. Tabera**
> Prefect
>
> † **A. Bugnini**
> Titular Archbishop of Diocletiana
> Secretary

---

[1] Second Vatican Council, constitution *Sacrosanctum Concilium* 75: *AAS* 56 (1964) 119.

[2] See *ibid*. 74: *loc. cit.*

APOSTOLIC CONSTITUTION

THE SACRAMENT OF ANOINTING
OF THE SICK

PAUL, BISHOP

Servant of the Servants of God

For Everlasting Memory

The Catholic Church professes and teaches that the anointing of the sick is one of the seven sacraments of the New Testament instituted by Christ and that it is "alluded to in Mark (6:13) and recommended and promulgated to the faithful by James the Apostle and brother of the Lord. He says: 'Is there anyone sick among you? Let him call for the elders of the Church, and let them pray over him and anoint him in the name of the Lord. This prayer, made in faith, will save the sick man. The Lord will restore his health, and if he has committed any sins, they will be forgiven' (James 5:14-15)." [1]

From ancient times testimonies of anointing of the sick have been found in the Church's tradition, particularly in the liturgy, both in the East and in the West. The letter which Innocent I, our predecessor, addressed to Decentius, Bishop of Gubbio,[2] and the venerable prayer used for blessing the oil of the sick: "Send forth, Lord, your Holy Spirit, the Paraclete," which was inserted in the eucharistic prayer[3] and is still preserved in the Roman Pontifical,[4] are worthy of special note.

In the course of centuries of liturgical tradition, the parts of the sick person's body to be anointed with holy oil were more explicitly defined in different ways. Several formulas were added to accompany the anointings with prayer, and

3

these are contained in the liturgical books of various churches. During the Middle Ages, in the Roman Church the custom prevailed of anointing the sick on the five senses with the formula: *"Per istam sanctam Unctionem, et suam piissimam misericordiam, indulgeat tibi Dominus quidquid deliquisti,"* adapted to each sense.[5]

In addition, the teaching concerning anointing is expounded in the documents of the ecumenical councils, namely, Florence, Trent especially, and Vatican II.

After the Council of Florence had described the essential elements of the anointing of the sick,[6] the Council of Trent declared its divine institution and explained what is taught in the Letter of James concerning the holy anointing, especially with regard to the reality and effects of the sacrament: "This reality is in fact the grace of the Holy Spirit, whose anointing takes away sins, if any still remain to be taken away, and the remnants of sin; it also relieves and strengthens the soul of the sick person, arousing in him a great confidence in the divine mercy; thus sustained, he may more easily bear the trials and hardships of his sickness, more easily resist the temptations of the devil 'lying in wait' (Genesis 3:15), and sometimes regain bodily health, if this is expedient for the health of the soul."[7] The same council also declared that these words of the Apostle state with sufficient clarity that "this anointing is to be administered to the sick, especially those who are in such a condition as to appear to have reached the end of their life, whence it is also called the sacrament of the dying."[8] Finally, it declared that the priest is the proper minister of the sacrament.[9]

The Second Vatican Council adds the following: " *'Extreme Unction,'* which may also and more fittingly be called 'anointing of the sick,' is not a sacrament for those only who are at the point of death. Hence, as soon as any one of the faithful begins to be in danger of death from sickness or old age, the appropriate time for him to receive this sacrament has certainly already arrived."[10] The use of this sacrament is a concern of the whole Church: "By the sacred anointing of the sick and the prayer of her priests, the whole Church commends the sick to the suffering and glorified Lord, asking that he may lighten their suffering and save them (see James 5:14-16). The Church exhorts them, moreover, to contribute to the welfare of the whole people of God by associating themselves freely with the passion and death of Christ (see Romans 8:17; Colossians 1:24; 2 Timothy 2:11-12; 1 Peter 4:13)."[11]

All these considerations had to be weighed in revising the rite of anointing, in order better to adapt to present day conditions those elements which were subject to change.[12]

We thought fit to modify the sacramental formula in such a way that, in view of the words of James, the effects of the sacrament might be more fully expressed.

Since olive oil, which had been prescribed until now for the valid administration of the sacrament, is unobtainable or difficult to obtain in some parts of the world, we decreed, at the request of numerous bishops, that from now on, according to the circumstances, another kind of oil could also be used, provided that it be obtained from plants, and thus similar to olive oil.

As regards the number of anointings and the parts of the body to be anointed, it has seemed opportune to simplify the rite.

Therefore, since this revision in certain points touches upon the sacramental rite itself, by our apostolic authority we lay down that the following is to be observed for the future in the Latin Rite:

The sacrament of anointing of the sick is administered to those who are dangerously ill by anointing them on the forehead and hands with blessed olive oil or, according to the circumstances, with another plant oil and saying once only these words: *"Per istam Sanctam Unctionem et suam piissi-*

*mam misericordiam adiuvet te Dominus gratia Spiritus Sancti,
ut a peccatis liberatum te salvet atque propitius allevet."*

In case of necessity, however, it is sufficient that a single anointing be given on the forehead or, because of the particular condition of the sick person, on another more suitable part of the body, the whole formula being pronounced.

This sacrament may be repeated if the sick person recovers after anointing and then again falls ill or if, in the course of the same illness, the danger becomes more serious.

Having established and declared all these elements of the essential rite of the sacrament of anointing of the sick, by our apostolic authority we also approve the **Rite of Anointing and Pastoral Care of the Sick,** which has been revised by the Congregation for Divine Worship. At the same time, where necessary we derogate from the prescriptions of the Code of Canon Law or other laws hitherto in force or we abrogate them; other prescriptions and laws, which are neither abrogated nor changed by the abovementioned rite, remain valid and in force. The Latin edition of the rite containing the new form will come into force as soon as it is published; the vernacular editions, prepared by the episcopal conferences and confirmed by the Apostolic See, will come into force on the dates to be laid down by the individual conferences. The old rite may be used until December 31, 1973. From January 1, 1974, however, only the new rite is to be used by those concerned.

We intend that everything we have laid down and prescribed should be firm and effective in the Latin Rite, notwithstanding, where relevant, the apostolic constitutions and ordinances issued by our predecessors and other prescriptions, even if worthy of special mention.

Given in Rome at Saint Peter's on November 30, 1972, the tenth year of our pontificate.

Paul Pp. VI

[1] Council of Trent, Session XIV, *Extreme unction*, chapter 1 (cf. *ibid.*, canon 1); *CT*, VII, 1, 355-356; Denz.-Schön. 1695, 1716.

[2] Ep. *Si Instituta Ecclesiastica*, chapter 8: PL 20, 559–561; Denz.-Schön. 216.

[3] *Liber Sacramentorum Romanae AEclesiae Ordinis Anni Circuli*, ed. L. C. Mohlberg (*Rerum Ecclesiasticarum Documenta, Fontes,* IV), Rome, 1960, p. 61; *Le Sacramentaire Grégorien*, ed. J. Deshusses (*Spicilegium Friburgense*, 16) Fribourg, 1971, p. 172; see *La Tradition Apostolique de Saint Hippolyte*, ed. B. Botte (*Liturgiewissenschaftliche Quellen und Forschungen*, 39), Münster in W., 1963, pp. 18-19; *Le Grand Euchologe du Monastère Blanc*, ed. E. Lanne (*Patrologia Orientalis*, XXVIII, 2), Paris, 1958, pp. 392-395.

[4] See *Pontificale Romanum: Ordo benedicendi Oleum Catechumenorum et Infirmorum et conficiendi Chrisma*, Vatican City, 1971, pp. 11-12.

[5] See M. Andrieu, *Le Pontifical Romain au Moyen-Age*, t. 1, *Le Pontifical Romain du XIIe siècle (Studi e Testi, 86)*, Vatican City, 1938, pp. 267-268; t. 2, *Le Pontifical de la Curie Romaine au XIIIe siècle (Studi e Testi, 87)*, Vatican City, 1940, pp. 491-492.

[6] *Decr. pro Armeniis*, G. Hofmann, *Concilium Florentinum*, I-II, p. 130; Denz.-Schön. 1324 s.

[7] Council of Trent, Session XIV, *Extreme unction*, chapter 2: *CT*, VII, 1, 356; Denz.-Schön. 1696.

[8] *Ibid.*, chapter 3: *CT, ibid.;* Denz.-Schön. 1698.

[9] *Ibid.*, chapter 3, canon 4: *CT, ibid.*; Denz.-Schön. 1697, 1719.

[10] Second Vatican Council, constitution *Sacrosanctum Concilium* 73: AAS 56 (1964) 118-119.

[11] *Ibid.*, constitution *Lumen gentium* 11: AAS 67 (1965) 15.

[12] See *ibid.*, constitution *Sacrosanctum Concilium* 1: AAS 56 (1964) 97.

RITE OF ANOINTING AND PASTORAL CARE OF THE SICK

INTRODUCTION

I. Human Sickness and Its Meaning in the Mystery of Salvation

1. Sickness and pain have always been a heavy burden for man and an enigma to his understanding. Christians suffer sickness and pain as do all other men; yet their faith helps them to understand better the mystery of suffering and to bear their pain more bravely. From Christ's words they know that sickness has meaning and value for their own salvation and for the world's; they also know that Christ loved the sick and that during his life he often looked upon the sick and healed them.

2. Sickness, while it is closely related to man's sinful condition, cannot be considered a punishment which man suffers for his personal sins (see John 9:3). Christ himself was sinless, yet he fulfilled what was written in Isaiah: he bore all the sufferings of his passion and understood human sorrow (see Isaiah 53:4-5). Christ still suffers and is tormented in his followers whenever we suffer. If we realize that our sufferings are preparing us for eternal life in glory, then they will seem short and even easy to bear (see 2 Corinthians 4:17).

3. It is part of the plan laid down by God's providence that we should struggle against all sickness and carefully seek the blessings of good health, so that we can fulfill our role in human society and in the Church. Yet we should always be prepared to fill up what is lacking in Christ's sufferings for the salvation of the world as we look forward to all creation being set free in the glory of the sons of God (see Colossians 1:24; Romans 8:19-21).

Moreover, the role of the sick in the Church is to remind others not to lose sight of the essential or higher things and so to show that our mortal life is restored through the mystery of Christ's death and resurrection.

4. Not only the sick person should fight against illness; doctors and all who are dedicated to helping the sick should consider it their duty to do whatever they judge will help the sick both physically and spiritually. In doing so they fulfill the command of Christ to visit the sick, for Christ implied that they should be concerned for the whole man and offer both physical relief and spiritual comfort.

II. Celebration of the Sacraments of the Sick

A. Anointing of the Sick

5. The sacrament of anointing prolongs the concern which the Lord himself showed for the bodily and spiritual welfare of the sick, as the gospels testify, and which he asked his followers to show also. This sacrament has its beginning in Christ and is spoken of in the Letter of James: the Church, by the anointing of the sick and the prayer of the priests, commends those who are ill to the suffering and glorified Lord, that he may raise them up and save them (see James 5:14-16). Moreover, the Church exhorts them to contribute to the welfare of the people of God[1] by associating themselves freely with the passion and death of Christ (see Romans 8:17).[2]

The man who is seriously ill needs the special help of God's grace in this time of anxiety, lest he be broken in spirit and subject to temptations and the weakening of faith.

Christ, therefore, strengthens the faithful who are afflicted by illness with the sacrament of anointing, providing them with the strongest means of support.[3]

The celebration of this sacrament consists especially in the laying on of hands by the presbyters of the Church, their offering the prayer of faith, and the anointing of the sick with oil made holy by God's blessing. This rite signifies the grace of the sacrament and confers it.

6. This sacrament provides the sick person with the grace of the Holy Spirit by which the whole man is brought to health, trust in God is encouraged, and strength is given to resist the temptations of the Evil One and anxiety about death. Thus the sick person is able not only to bear his suffering bravely, but also to fight against it. A return to physical health may even follow the reception of this sacrament if it will be beneficial to the sick person's salvation. If necessary, the sacrament also provides the sick person with the forgiveness of sins and the completion of Christian penance.[4]

7. The anointing of the sick, which includes the prayer of faith (see James 5:15), is a sacrament of faith. This faith is important for the minister and particularly for the one who receives it. The sick man will be saved by his faith and the faith of the Church which looks back to the death and resurrection of Christ, the source of the sacrament's power (see James 5:15),[5] and looks ahead to the future kingdom which is pledged in the sacraments.

a) Subject of the Anointing of the Sick

8. The Letter of James states that the anointing should be given to the sick to raise them up and save them.[6] There should be special care and concern that those who are dangerously ill due to sickness or old age receive this sacra-ment.[7]

A prudent or probable judgment about the seriousness of the sickness is sufficient;[8] in such a case there is no reason for scruples, but if necessary a doctor may be consulted.

9. The sacrament may be repeated if the sick person recovers after anointing or if, during the same illness, the danger becomes more serious.

10. A sick person should be anointed before surgery whenever a dangerous illness is the reason for the surgery.

11. Old people may be anointed if they are in weak con-dition although no dangerous illness is present.

12. Sick children may be anointed if they have sufficient use of reason to be comforted by this sacrament.

13. In public and private catechesis, the faithful should be encouraged to ask for the anointing and, as soon as the time for the anointing comes, to receive it with complete faith and devotion, not misusing this sacrament by putting it off. All who care for the sick should be taught the meaning and purpose of anointing.

14. Anointing may be conferred upon sick people who have lost consciousness or lost the use of reason, if, as Christian believers, they would have asked for it were they in control of their faculties.[9]

15. When a priest has been called to attend a person who is already dead, he should pray for the dead person, asking that God forgive his sins and graciously receive him into his kingdom. The priest is not to administer the sacrament of anointing. But if the priest is doubtful whether the sick person is dead, he may administer the sacrament conditionally (no. 135).[10]

b) Minister of Anointing

16. The priest is the only proper minister of the anointing of the sick.[11]

This office is ordinarily exercised by bishops, pastors and their assistants, priests who care for the sick or aged in hospitals, and superiors of clerical religious institutions.

17. These ministers have the pastoral responsibility, with the assistance of religious and laity, first of preparing and helping the sick and others who are present, and then of celebrating the sacrament.

The local ordinary has the responsibility of supervising celebrations at which sick persons from various parishes or hospitals come together to receive the anointing.

18. Other priests, with the consent of the ministers mentioned in no. 16, may confer the anointing. In case of necessity, a priest may presume this consent, but he should later inform the pastor or the chaplain of the hospital.

19. When two or more priests are present for the anointing of a sick person, one of them says the prayers and performs the anointings, saying the sacramental form. The others take various parts such as the introductory rites, readings, invocations or explanations; they may each lay hands on the sick person.

c) Requirements for Celebrating the Anointing of the Sick

20. The matter proper for the sacrament is olive oil, or according to circumstances, other plant oil.[13]

21. The oil used for anointing the sick must be blessed for this purpose by the bishop or by a priest who has this faculty, either from the law or by special concession of the Apostolic See.

The law itself permits the following to bless the oil of the sick:

a) those whom the law equates with diocesan bishops;
b) in case of true necessity, any priest.[14]

The oil of the sick is ordinarily blessed by the bishop on Holy Thursday.[15]

22. If a priest, according to no. 21b, is to bless the oil during the rite, he may bring the unblessed oil with him, or the family of the sick person may prepare the oil in a suitable vessel. If any of the oil is left after the celebration of the sacrament, it should be absorbed in cotton and burned.

If the priest uses oil that has already been blessed (either by the bishop or by a priest), he brings it with him in the vessel in which it is kept. This vessel, made of a suitable material, should be clean and should contain sufficient oil (soaked in cotton for convenience). In this case, after the anointing the priest returns the vessel to the place where it is reverently kept. He should make sure that the oil remains fit for use and should obtain fresh oil from time to time, either yearly when the bishop blesses the oil on Holy Thursday or more frequently if necessary.

23. The sacrament is conferred by anointing the sick person on the forehead and on the hands. The formula is divided so that the first part is said while the forehead is anointed, the latter part while the hands are anointed.

In case of necessity, however, a single anointing on the forehead is enough. If the condition of the sick person prevents anointing the forehead, another suitable part of the body is anointed. In either case, the whole formula is said.

24. Depending on the culture and traditions of different peoples, the number of anointings and the place of anointing may be changed or increased. Provision for this should be made in the preparation of particular rituals.

25. The following is the formula with which the anointing of the sick is conferred in the Latin Rite:

Through this holy anointing
may the Lord in his love and mercy help you
with the grace of the Holy Spirit.
May the Lord who frees you from sin
save you and raise you up.

B. Viaticum

26. When the Christian, in his passage from this life, is strengthened by the body and blood of Christ, he has the pledge of the resurrection which the Lord promised: "He who eats my flesh and drinks my blood has eternal life, and I will raise him up at the last day" (John 6:54).

Viaticum should be received during Mass when possible so that the sick person may receive communion under both kinds. Communion received as viaticum should be considered a special sign of participation in the mystery of the death of the Lord and his passage to the Father,[16] the mystery which is celebrated in the eucharist.

27. All baptized Christians who can receive communion are bound to receive viaticum. Those in danger of death from any cause are obliged to receive communion. Pastors must see that the administration of this sacrament is not delayed, but that the faithful are nourished by it while still in full possession of their faculties.[17]

28. It is also desirable that, during the celebration of viaticum, the Christian should renew the faith he professed in baptism, which made him an adopted son of God and a co-heir of the promise of eternal life.

29. The ordinary ministers of viaticum are the pastor and his assistants, the priest who cares for the sick in hospitals, and the superior of clerical religious institutes. In case of necessity, any other priest, with at least the presumed permission of the competent minister, may administer viaticum.

If no priest is available, viaticum may be brought to the sick by a deacon or by another of the faithful, either a man or a woman who by the authority of the Apostolic See has been appointed by the bishop to distribute the eucharist to the faithful. In this case, a deacon follows the rite prescribed in the ritual; other ministers use the rite they ordinarily follow for distributing communion, but with the special formula given in the rite for viaticum (no. 112).

C. Continuous Rite

30. For special cases, when sudden illness or some other cause has unexpectedly placed one of the faithful in danger of death, a continuous rite is provided by which the sick person may be given the sacraments of penance, anointing, and the eucharist as viaticum in one service.

If death is near and there is not enough time to administer the three sacraments in the manner described above, the sick person should be given an opportunity to make a sacramental confession, which of necessity may be a generic confession. Then, he should be given viaticum immediately, since all the faithful are bound by precept to receive this sacrament if they are in danger of death. Afterwards, if there is sufficient time, the sick person is to be anointed.

If because of his illness the sick person cannot receive communion, he should be anointed.

31. If the sick person is to receive the sacrament of confirmation, nos. 117, 124, and 136-137 of this ritual should be consulted.

In danger of death, provided a bishop is not easily available or is lawfully impeded, the law gives the faculty to confirm to the following: pastors and parochial vicars; in their absence, their parochial associates; priests who are in charge of special parishes lawfully established; administrators, substitutes, and assistants; in the absence of all of the preceding, any priest who is not subject to censure or canonical penalty.[18]

III. Offices and Ministries for the Sick

32. If one member suffers in the body of Christ, which is the Church, all the members suffer with him (1 Corinthians 12:26).[19] For this reason, kindness shown toward the sick and works of charity and mutual help for the relief of every kind of human want should be held in special honor.[20] Every scientific effort to prolong life[21] and every act of heartfelt love for the sick may be considered a preparation for the gospel and a participation in Christ's healing ministry.[22]

33. It is thus fitting that all baptized Christians share in this ministry of mutual charity within the body of Christ: by fighting against disease, by love shown to the sick, and by celebrating the sacraments of the sick. Like the other sacraments, these too have a communal aspect, which should be brought out as much as possible when they are celebrated.

34. The family and friends of the sick and those who take care of them have a special share in this ministry of comfort. It is their task to strengthen the sick with words of faith and by praying with them, to commend them to the Lord who suffered and is glorified, and to urge the sick to unite themselves willingly with the passion and death of Christ for the good of God's people.[23] If the sickness grows worse, the family and friends of the sick and those who take care of them have the responsibility to inform the pastor and by their kind words prudently to dispose the sick person for the reception of the sacraments at the proper time.

35. Priests, particularly pastors and those mentioned in no. 16, should remember that they are to care for the sick, visiting them and helping them by works of charity.[24] Especially when they administer the sacraments, priests should stir up the hope of those present and strengthen their faith in Christ who suffered and was glorified. By expressing the Church's love and the consolation of faith, they should comfort believers and raise the minds of others to God.

36. The faithful should clearly understand the meaning of the anointing of the sick so that these sacraments may nourish, strengthen, and express faith. It is most important for the faithful in general, and above all for the sick, to be aided by suitable instructions in preparing for this celebration and in participating in it, especially if it is to be carried out communally. The prayer of faith which accompanies the celebration of the sacrament is supported by the profession of this faith.

37. When the priest prepares for the celebration of the sacraments, he should ask about the condition of the sick person. He should take this information into account when he arranges the rite, in choosing readings and prayers, in deciding whether he will celebrate Mass for viaticum, and the like. As far as possible he should plan all this with the sick person or his family beforehand, while he explains the meaning of the sacraments.

IV. Adaptations by the Conferences of Bishops

38. According to the Constitution on the Liturgy (no. 63b), it is for the conferences of bishops to prepare a title in particular rituals corresponding to this title of the Roman Ritual. It should be accommodated to the needs of the region so that, after the decisions have been reviewed by the Apostolic See, the ritual can be used in the region for which it was prepared.

The following pertains to the episcopal conferences:

a) to specify adaptations, as mentioned in no. 39 of the Constitution on the Liturgy;

b) carefully and prudently to consider what can properly be accepted from the genius and the traditions of each nation; to propose to the Apostolic See further adaptations which seem useful or necessary and to introduce them with its consent;

c) to retain elements in the rites of the sick which now exist in particular rituals, so long as they are compatible with the Constitution on the Liturgy and with contemporary needs; or to adapt any of these elements;

d) to prepare translations of the texts so that they are truly accommodated to the genius of different languages and cultures, with the addition of melodies for singing when this is appropriate;

e) to adapt and enlarge, if necessary, the introduction given in the Roman Ritual so as to encourage the conscious and active participation of the faithful;

f) to arrange the material in the editions of liturgical books prepared under the direction of the episcopal conferences so that they will be suitable for pastoral use.

39. Wherever the Roman Ritual gives several optional formulas, particular rituals may add other texts of the same kind.

V. Adaptations by the Minister

40. The minister should be aware of particular circumstances and other needs, as well as the wishes of the sick and of other members of the faithful, and should freely use the different options provided in the rite.

a) He should be especially aware that the sick tire easily and that their physical condition can change from day to day and even from hour to hour. For this reason he may shorten the rite if necessary.

b) When the faithful are not present, the priest should remember that the Church is already present in his own person and in the person of the one who is ill. For this reason he should try to offer the sick person the love and help of the Christian community both before and after the celebration of the sacrament, or he may ask another Christian from the local community to do this if the sick person will accept this help.

c) If the sick person regains his health after being anointed, he should be encouraged to give thanks for the favors he has received, for example, by participating in a Mass of thanksgiving or in some other suitable manner.

41. The priest should follow the structure of the rite in the celebration, while accommodating it to the place and the people involved. The penitential rite may be part of the introductory rite or take place after the reading from scripture. In place of the thanksgiving over the oil, the priest may give an instruction. This is particularly appropriate when the sick person is in a hospital and the other sick people in the room do not take part in the celebration of the sacrament.

---

[1] See Council of Trent, Session XIV, *Extreme unction*, chapter 1: Denz.-Schön. 1695; Second Vatican Council, constitution *Lumen gentium*, no. 11: *AAS* 57 (1965) 15.

[2] See also Colossians 1:24; 2 Timothy 2:11-12; 1 Peter 4:13.

[3] See Council of Trent, Session XIV, *loc. cit.*: Denz.-Schön. 1694.

[4] See *ibid.*, foreword and chapter 2: Denz.-Schön. 1694 and 1696.

[5] See St. Thomas, *In IV Sententiarum*, d. 1. q. 1, a. 4. qc. 3.

[6] See Council of Trent, Session XIV, *Extreme unction*, chapter 2: Denz.-Schön. 1698.

[7] See Second Vatican Council, constitution *Sacrosanctum Concilium*, no. 73: *AAS* 56 (1964) 118-119.

[8] See Pius XI, Letter *Explorata res*, February 2, 1923.

[9] See canon 943, C.I.C.

[10] See canon 941, C.I.C.

[11] See Council of Trent, Session XIV, *Extreme unction*, chapter 3 and canon 4: Denz.-Schön. 1697 and 1719; canon 938, C.I.C.

[12] See canon 938, C.I.C.

[13] See *Ordo benedicendi Oleum catechumenorum et infirmorum et conficiendi Chrisma*, Praenotanda, no. 3, Vatican Press, 1970.

[14] *Ibid*., introduction, no. 8.

[15] *Ibid*., introduction, no. 9.

[16] See S.R.C., instruction *Eucharisticum Mysterium*, May 25, 1967, nos. 36, 39, 41: *AAS* 59 (1967) 561, 562, 563; Paul VI, apostolic letter *Pastorale munus*, November 30, 1963, no. 7: *AAS* 56 (1964) 7; canon 822, §4, C.I.C.

[17] See S.R.C., *Eucharisticum Mysterium*, no. 39: *AAS* 59 (1967) 562.

[18] See *Ordo Confirmationis*, Praenotanda, no. 7c, Vatican Press, 1971.

[19] See Second Vatican Council, constitution *Lumen gentium*, no. 7: *AAS* 57 (1965) 9-10.

[20] See Second Vatican Council, decree *Apostolicam actuositatem*, no. 8: *AAS* 58 (1966) 845.

[21] See Second Vatican Council, constitution *Gaudium et spes*, no. 18: *AAS* 58 (1966) 1038.

[22] See Second Vatican Council, constitution *Lumen gentium*, no. 28: *AAS* 57 (1965) 34.

[23] See *ibid*., no. 21.

[24] See canon 468, §1, C.I.C.

CHAPTER I

VISITATION AND COMMUNION OF THE SICK

I. VISITING THE SICK

42. All Christians should share in the care and love of Christ and the Church for the sick and should show their concern for them, as much as each one is able, by visiting them and comforting them in the Lord, offering them fraternal help in their need.

43. Pastors especially and others who care for the sick should offer them words of faith and explain the significance of human suffering in the mystery of salvation. They should also urge the sick to realize that through their faith they are united with Christ's suffering and that with prayer they can sanctify their sickness and draw strength to bear their suffering.

It is the special task of priests to lead the sick step by step to the sacraments of penance and the eucharist, which they should receive often if their condition permits, and, in particular, to the sacraments of anointing and viaticum at the appropriate times.

44. The sick should be encouraged to pray when they are alone or with their families, friends, or those who care for them. Their prayer should draw primarily upon the scriptures, by meditating on those parts which speak of the mystery of human suffering in Christ and in his works or by using prayers drawn from the psalms and other texts. The sick should be helped in making this sort of prayer, and priests should always be ready to pray with them.

45. When visiting the sick, the priest may choose, together with the sick person and those present, suitable elements of common prayer in the form of a brief liturgy of the word. As the occasion permits, prayer drawn from the psalms or from other prayers or litanies should be added to the word of God. At the end the sick person should be blessed, and, depending on his condition, the laying on of hands may be added.

II. COMMUNION OF THE SICK

46. Pastors should see to it that the sick and aged, even if not seriously sick or in imminent danger of death, be given every opportunity to receive the eucharist frequently and even daily, if possible, especially during the Easter season. They may receive communion at any hour.

A sick person who is unable to receive the eucharist under the form of bread may receive communion under the form of wine alone, in accord with no. 95.

Those who care for the sick may also receive communion with them, the requirements of the law being observed.

47. In bringing the eucharist for communion outside the church, the sacred species should be carried in a pyx or other small closed container; the attire of the minister and the manner of carrying the eucharist should be appropriate to the local circumstances.

48. Those who live with or take care of the sick person should be instructed to prepare a table covered with a linen cloth in the bedroom, upon which the sacrament is to be placed. If customary, a vessel of holy water and a sprinkler or a small branch should be provided, as well as candles.

ORDINARY RITE OF COMMUNION OF THE SICK

Greeting

49. Wearing the appropriate vestments, the priest approaches the sick person and greets him and the others present in a friendly manner. He may use this greeting:

A **Peace to this house and to all who live in it.**

B **The peace of the Lord be with you.**

[230]

C **The grace of our Lord Jesus Christ and the love of God and the fellowship of the Holy Spirit be with you all.**

R̸. **And also with you.**

[231]

D **The grace and peace of God our Father and the Lord Jesus Christ be with you.**

R̸. **Blessed be God the Father of our Lord Jesus Christ.**

Or:

R̸. **And also with you.**

Then he places the sacrament on the table, and all adore it.

Sprinkling with Holy Water

50.   According to the circumstances, the priest may sprinkle the sick person and the room with holy water, saying the following words or those given in a particular ritual:

**Let this water call to mind
your baptismal sharing
in Christ's redeeming passion and resurrection.**

Penitential Rite

51.   If necessary, the priest hears the sick person's sacramental confession.

52.   When sacramental confession is not part of the rite or if there are others to receive communion, the priest invites the sick person and all present to join in the penitential rite:

My brothers and sisters, to prepare ourselves for this celebration, let us call to mind our sins.

After a brief silence, all say:

**I confess to almighty God,
and to you, my brothers and sisters,
that I have sinned through my own fault**

They strike their breast:

**in my thoughts and in my words,
in what I have done,
and in what I have failed to do;**

and I ask blessed Mary, ever Virgin,
all the angels and saints,
and you, my brothers and sisters,
to pray for me to the Lord our God.

A The priest concludes:

**May almighty God have mercy on us,
forgive us our sins,
and bring us to everlasting life.**

All answer: **Amen.**

Other forms of the penitential rite may be chosen:

[232]

After a brief silence, the priest says:

**Lord, we have sinned against you:
Lord, have mercy.**

All answer: **Lord, have mercy.**

B Priest: **Lord, show us your mercy and love.**

All answer: **And grant us your salvation.**

The priest concludes:

**May almighty God have mercy on us,
forgive us our sins,
and bring us to everlasting life.**

All answer: **Amen.**

[233]

After a brief silence, the priest or one of the others present says the following or other invocations with the Kyrie:

You brought us to salvation by your paschal mystery:
Lord, have mercy.

All: **Lord, have mercy.**

Priest: **You renew us by the wonders of your passion:**
Christ, have mercy.

All: **Christ, have mercy.**

Priest: **You make us sharers in your paschal sacrifice**
by our partaking of your body:
Lord, have mercy.

All: **Lord, have mercy.**

The priest concludes:

May almighty God have mercy on us,
forgive us our sins,
and bring us to everlasting life.

All: **Amen.**

Reading from Scripture

53.   A text from the scriptures may then be read by one of those present or by the priest. For example:

John 6:54-55 or John 6:54-59

A
"He who eats my flesh
and drinks my blood has eternal life,
and I will raise him up at the last day.
For my flesh is food indeed,
and my blood is drink indeed.
[He who eats my flesh and drinks my blood
abides in me, and I in him.
As the living Father sent me,
and I live because of the Father,
so he who eats me will live because of me.
This is the bread which came down from heaven,
not such as the fathers ate and died;
he who eats this bread will live for ever."
This he said in the synagogue,
as he taught at Capernaum.]"

John 14:6

B
Jesus said,
"I am the way, and the truth, and the life;
no one comes to the Father, but by me."

John 14:23

C
Jesus answered,
"If a man loves me,
he will keep my word,
and my Father will love him,
and we will come to him
and make our home with him."

John 15:4

"Abide in me, and I in you.
As the branch cannot bear fruit by itself,
unless it abides in the vine,
neither can you,
unless you abide in me."

1 Corinthians 11:26

For as often as you eat this bread and drink the
cup, you proclaim the Lord's death until he comes.

John 14:27

"Peace I leave with you;
my peace I give to you;
not as the world gives do I give to you.
Let not your hearts be troubled,
neither let them be afraid."

John 15:5

"I am the vine, you are the branches.
He who abides in me, and I in him,
he it is that bears much fruit,
for apart from me you can do nothing."

1 John 4:16

We know and believe the love God has for us.
God is love,
and he who abides in love abides in God,
and God abides in him.

The priest may then briefly explain the text.

Lord's Prayer

54.   The priest introduces the Lord's Prayer in these or similar words:

**Now let us pray to God as our Lord Jesus Christ
taught us.**

All continue:

**Our Father, who art in heaven,
hallowed be thy name;
thy kingdom come;
thy will be done on earth as it is in heaven.
Give us this day our daily bread;
and forgive us our trespasses
as we forgive those who trespass against us;
and lead us not into temptation,
but deliver us from evil.**

Communion

55.   Then the priest shows the holy eucharist to those present, saying:

**This is the Lamb of God
who takes away the sins of the world.
Happy are those who are called to his supper.**

The sick person and all who are to receive communion say once:

**Lord, I am not worthy to receive you,
but only say the word and I shall be healed.**

56.   The priest goes to the sick person and, showing him the sacrament, says:

The body of Christ (or: **The blood of Christ**).

The sick person answers: **Amen,** and receives communion.

Others present then receive communion in the usual manner.

57. After communion the minister washes the vessel as usual. Then a period of sacred silence may be observed.

Concluding Rite

The priest says the concluding prayer:

Let us pray.

God our Father, almighty and eternal,
we confidently call upon you,
that the body [and blood] of Christ
which our brother (sister) has received
may bring him (her)
lasting health in mind and body.

We ask this through Christ our Lord.

℟. **Amen.**

[234]

Father,
you brought to completion
the work of our redemption
through the paschal mystery of Christ your Son.
May we who faithfully proclaim

his death and resurrection
in these sacramental signs
experience the constant growth of your salvation
B   in our lives.

We ask this through Christ our Lord.

℟. Amen.

[235]

God our Father,
you give us a share in the one bread and the one
   cup
and make us one in Christ.
C May our lives bring your salvation and joy
to all the world.

We ask this through Christ our Lord.

℟. Amen.

[236]

Lord,
in the eucharist we share today
you renew our life.
D Through your Spirit,
make your life grow strong within us
and keep us faithful to you.

We ask this in the name of Jesus the Lord.

℟. Amen.

Blessing

58. The priest then blesses the sick person and
the others present, either by making the sign of the

cross over them with the pyx, if any of the sacrament remains, or by using one of the forms of
blessing given in the rites for the sick (nos. 79,
237, or 238) or the blessing at the end of Mass:

May God the Father bless you.   [79]

℟. **Amen.**

May God the Son heal you.

℟. **Amen.**

May God the Holy Spirit enlighten you.

℟. **Amen.**

**May God protect you from harm
and grant you salvation.**

℟. **Amen.**

**May he shine on your heart
and lead you to eternal life.**

℟. **Amen.**

**[And may almighty God,
the Father, and the Son, ✝ and the Holy Spirit,
bless you all.**

℟. **Amen.]**

                                                     [237]

**May the Lord Jesus Christ be with you to protect
you.**

℟. **Amen.**

**May he go before you to guide you
and stand behind you to give you strength.**

℟. **Amen.**

May he look upon you, to keep you and bless you.

B

℟. **Amen.**

**[And may almighty God,
the Father, and the Son, ✝ and the Holy Spirit,
bless you all.**

℟. **Amen.]**

[238]

C

**May the blessing of almighty God,
the Father, and the Son, ✝ and the Holy Spirit,
come upon you and remain with you for ever.**

℟. **Amen.**

SHORT RITE OF COMMUNION OF THE SICK

59. This shorter rite is to be used when communion is given in different rooms of the same building, such as a hospital. Elements taken from the ordinary rite may be added according to circumstances.

60. If the sick persons wish to confess, the priest hears their confessions and absolves them at a convenient time before he begins the distribution of communion.

61. The rite may begin in the church or chapel or in the first room, where the priest says the following antiphon or one given in a particular ritual:

**Through this holy meal,
in which Christ is received,
the memorial of his passion is recalled,
our lives are filled with grace,
and a promise of future glory is given to us.**

62. The priest may be escorted by a person carrying a candle. He says to all the sick persons in the same room or to each communicant individually:

**This is the Lamb of God
who takes away the sins of the world.
Happy are those who are called to his supper.**

The one who is to receive communion then says once:

**Lord, I am not worthy to receive you,
but only say the word and I shall be healed.**

He receives communion in the usual manner.

63. The concluding prayer may be said either in the church or chapel or in the last room; the blessing is omitted.

Let us pray.

[57]

A

**God our Father, almighty and eternal,
we confidently call upon you,
that the body [and blood] of Christ
which our brothers [and sisters] have received
may bring them
lasting health in mind and body.
We ask this through Christ our Lord.**

℟. **Amen.**

[234]

B

**Father,
you have brought to completion
the work of our redemption
through the paschal mystery of Christ your Son.
May we who faithfully proclaim
his death and resurrection
in these sacramental signs
experience the constant growth of your salvation
    in our lives.
We ask this through Christ our Lord.**

℟. **Amen.**

[235]

God our Father,
you give us a share in the one bread and the one
** cup**

C **and make us one in Christ.**
May our lives bring your salvation and joy
to all the world.
We ask this through Christ our Lord.

℟. **Amen.**

[236]

Lord,
in the eucharist we share today
you renew our life.

D **Through your Spirit,**
make your life grow strong within us
and keep us faithful to you.
We ask this in the name of Jesus the Lord.

℟. **Amen.**

CHAPTER II

RITE OF ANOINTING A SICK PERSON

ORDINARY RITE

Preparation for the Celebration

64. Before he anoints a sick person, the priest should inquire about his condition in order to plan the celebration properly and to choose the biblical readings and the prayers. If possible he should make this preparation with the sick person or his family, while explaining to them the significance of the sacrament.

65. Whenever it is necessary, the priest should hear the sacramental confession of the sick person, if possible, before the celebration of the anointing. If the person confesses at the time of the anointing, this takes place during the introductory rite. Otherwise the penitential rite should be celebrated.

66. The sick person who is not confined to bed may receive the sacrament of anointing in the church or some other appropriate place. A suitable chair or place should be prepared, and there should be room for his relatives and friends to take part.

In hospitals the priest should consider the other sick people: whether they are able to take part in the celebration, whether they are very weak, or, if they are not Catholics, whether they might be offended.

67. The rite described below may also be used for anointing several sick persons at the same time. In this case, the priest lays hands on each one individually and anoints each one, using the appointed form. Everything else is done once for all, and the prayers are recited in the plural.

Introductory Rites

68. Wearing the appropriate vestments, the priest approaches the sick person and greets him and the others present in a friendly manner. He may use this greeting:

A **Peace to this house and to all who live in it.**

B **The peace of the Lord be with you.**

[230]

C **The grace of our Lord Jesus Christ and the love of God and the fellowship of the Holy Spirit be with you all.**

℟. **And also with you.**

[231]

D **The grace and peace of God our Father and the Lord Jesus Christ be with you.**

℟. **Blessed be God the Father of our Lord Jesus Christ.**

D

Or:

℟. **And also with you.**

Then he places the sacrament on the table, and all adore it.

69. According to the circumstances, the priest may sprinkle the sick person and the room with holy water, saying the following words or those given in a particular ritual:

**Let this water call to mind
your baptismal sharing
in Christ's redeeming passion and resurrection.**

70. Then he addresses those present in these or similar words:

Dear brothers and sisters.

A

We have come together in the name of our Lord Jesus Christ, who restored the sick to health, and who himself suffered so much for our sake. He is present among us as we recall the words of the apostle James: "Is there anyone sick among you? Let him call for the elders of the Church, and let them pray over him and anoint him in the name of the Lord. This prayer, made in faith, will save the sick man. The Lord will restore his health, and if he has committed any sins, they will be forgiven."

Let us entrust our sick brother (sister) N. to the grace and power of Jesus Christ, that the Lord

A may ease his (her) suffering and grant him (her) health and salvation.

Or he may say the following prayer [no. 239]:

Lord God,
you have told us through your apostle James:
"Is there anyone sick among you?
Let him call for the elders of the Church,
and let them pray over him
and anoint him in the name of the Lord.
This prayer, made in faith, will save the sick man.
The Lord will restore his health,
B and if he has committed any sins,
they will be forgiven."

Gathered here in your name,
we ask you to listen to the prayer we make in faith:
in your love and kindness,
protect our brother (sister) N. in his (her) illness
[and all the sick here present].
Lead us all to the peace and joy of your kingdom
where you live for ever and ever.

℟. Amen.

Penitential Rite

71. If there is no sacramental confession, the penitential rite then follows. The priest begins in this manner:

My brothers and sisters, to prepare ourselves for this holy anointing, let us call to mind our sins.

After a brief silence, all say:

**I confess to almighty God,
and to you, my brothers and sisters,
that I have sinned through my own fault**

They strike their breast:

**in my thoughts and in my words,
in what I have done,
and in what I have failed to do;
and I ask blessed Mary, ever Virgin,
all the angels and saints,
and you, my brothers and sisters,
to pray for me to the Lord our God.**

The priest concludes:

**May almighty God have mercy on us,
forgive us our sins,
and bring us to everlasting life.**

All answer: **Amen.**

[232]

After a brief silence, the priest says:

**Lord, we have sinned against you:
Lord, have mercy.**

All answer: **Lord, have mercy.**

Priest: **Lord, show us your mercy and love.**

All answer: **And grant us your salvation.**

The priest concludes:

B

**May almighty God have mercy on us,
forgive us our sins,
and bring us to everlasting life.**

All answer: **Amen.**

[233]

After a brief silence, the priest or one of the others present says the following or other invocations with the Kyrie:

**You brought us to salvation by your paschal mystery:
Lord, have mercy.**

All: **Lord, have mercy.**

C

Priest: **You renew us by the wonders of your passion:
Christ, have mercy.**

All: **Christ, have mercy.**

Priest: **You make us sharers in your paschal sacrifice
by our partaking of your body:
Lord, have mercy.**

All: **Lord, have mercy.**

The priest concludes:

May almighty God have mercy on us,
forgive us our sins,
C
and bring us to everlasting life.

All: **Amen.**

Reading from Scripture

72. Then a brief text from scripture is read by one of those present or by the priest:

Brothers and sisters, listen to the words of the gospel according to Matthew (Matthew 8:5-10, 13).

As Jesus entered Capernaum, a centurion came forward to him, beseeching him and saying, "Lord, my servant is lying paralyzed at home, in terrible distress." And he said to him, "I will come and heal him." But the centurion answered him, "Lord, I am not worthy to have you come under my roof; but only say the word, and my servant will be healed. For I am a man under authority, with soldiers under me; and I say to one, 'Go,' and he goes, and to another, 'Come,' and he comes, and to my slave, 'Do this,' and he does it." When Jesus heard him, he marveled, and said to those who followed him, "Truly, I say to you, not even in Israel have I found such faith." And to the centurion Jesus said, "Go; be it done for you as you have believed." And the servant was healed at that very moment.

Or some other suitable reading may be used, for example, nos. 153-229. Depending on circumstances, the priest may give a brief explanation of the text.

Litany

73. The following litany may be said here or after the anointing or even, according to circumstances, at some other point. The priest may adapt or shorten the text.

My brothers and sisters, with faith let us ask the Lord to hear our prayers for our brother (sister) N.

Lord, through this holy anointing, come and comfort N. with your love and mercy.

℞. **Lord, hear our prayer.**

Free N. from all harm.

℞. **Lord, hear our prayer.**

Relieve the sufferings of all the sick [here present].

℞. **Lord, hear our prayer.**

Assist all those dedicated to the care of the sick.

℞. **Lord, hear our prayer.**

Free N. from sin and all temptation.

℞. **Lord, hear our prayer.**

Give life and health to our brother (sister) N., on whom we lay our hands in your name.

℞. **Lord, hear our prayer.**

[240]

You bore our weakness and carried our sorrows:
Lord, have mercy.

℟. **Lord, have mercy.**

You felt compassion for the crowd,
and went among them doing good and healing the
B sick:
Christ, have mercy.

℟. **Christ, have mercy.**

You commanded your apostles
to lay their hands on the sick in your name:
Lord, have mercy.

℟. **Lord, have mercy.**

[241]

Let us pray to the Lord for our sick brother (sister)
and for all those dedicated to serving and caring
for him (her).

Look kindly on our sick brother (sister).

℟. **Lord, hear our prayer.**

C Give new strength to his (her) body and mind.

℟. **Lord, hear our prayer.**

Ease our brother's (sister's) sufferings.

℟. **Lord, hear our prayer.**

Free him (her) from sin and temptation.

℟. **Lord, hear our prayer.**

Sustain all the sick with your power.

℞. Lord, hear our prayer.

Assist all who care for the sick.

C

℞. Lord, hear our prayer.

Give life and health to our brother (sister),
on whom we lay our hands in your name.

℞. Lord, hear our prayer.

Laying on of Hands

74.   The priest then lays his hands on the head
of the sick person in silence.

Blessing of Oil

75.   When the priest is to bless the oil during
the rite, in accord with no. 21, he continues:

Let us pray.

Lord God, loving Father,
you bring healing to the sick
through your Son Jesus Christ.
Hear us as we pray to you in faith,

A

and send the Holy Spirit, man's Helper and Friend,
upon this oil, which nature has provided
to serve the needs of men.
May your blessing ✝
come upon all who are anointed with this oil,

that they may be freed from pain and illness
and made well again in body, mind, and soul.
Father, may this oil be blessed for our use
in the name of our Lord Jesus Christ
who lives and reigns with you for ever and ever.

℟. **Amen.**

[242]

Praise to you, almighty God and Father.
You sent your Son to live among us
and bring us salvation.

℟. **Blessed be God.**

Praise to you, Lord Jesus Christ,
the Father's only Son.
You humbled yourself to share in our humanity,
and desired to cure all our illnesses.

℟. **Blessed be God.**

Praise to you, God the Holy Spirit, the Consoler.
You heal our sickness with your mighty power.

℟. **Blessed be God.**

Lord,
mercifully listen to our prayers
and bless this oil intended to ease the sufferings
    of your people.
May those for whom we pray in faith
and who are anointed with this holy oil,
be freed from the illness that afflicts them.

We ask this through Christ our Lord.

℟. **Amen.**

Prayer of Thanksgiving

75b.   If the oil is already blessed, the priest says
the prayer of thanksgiving over it:

Praise to you, almighty God and Father.
You sent your Son to live among us and bring us
**   salvation.**

R̷. **Blessed be God.**

Praise to you, Lord Jesus Christ, the Father's only
**   Son.**
You humbled yourself to share in our humanity,
**   and you desired to cure all our illnesses.**

R̷. **Blessed be God.**

Praise to you, God the Holy Spirit, the Consoler.
You heal our sickness, with your mighty power.

R̷. **Blessed be God.**

Lord God,
with faith in you
our brother (sister) will be anointed with this holy
**   oil.**
Ease his (her) sufferings and strengthen him (her)
**   in his (her) weakness.**

We ask this through Christ our Lord.

R̷. **Amen.**

Anointing

76. Then the priest takes the oil and anoints the sick person on the forehead and the hands, saying once:

**Through this holy anointing
may the Lord in his love and mercy help you
with the grace of the Holy Spirit.**

℞. **Amen.**

**May the Lord who frees you from sin
save you and raise you up.**

℞. **Amen.**

Prayer after Anointing

77. Afterwards the priest says one of the following prayers:

Let us pray.

A
**Lord Jesus Christ, our Redeemer,
by the power of the Holy Spirit,
ease the sufferings of our sick brother (sister)
and make him (her) well again in mind and body.
In your loving kindness forgive his (her) sins
and grant him (her) full health
so that he (she) may be restored to your service.**

You are Lord for ever and ever.

℞. **Amen.**

B
**Lord Jesus Christ,
you shared in our human nature
to heal the sick and save all mankind.**

Mercifully listen to our prayers
for the physical and spiritual health of our sick
   brother (sister)
whom we have anointed in your name.

B May your protection console him (her)
and your strength make him (her) well again.
[Help him (her) find hope in suffering,
for you have given him (her) a share in your passion.]

You are Lord for ever and ever.

℞. Amen.

Other prayers suited to various conditions of the
sick:

[243]

   When the illness is the result of advanced age.

Lord,
look kindly on our brother (sister)
who has grown weak under the burden of his (her)
   years.
In this holy anointing
C he (she) asks for the grace of health in body and
   soul.
By the power of your Holy Spirit,
make him (her) firm in faith and sure in hope,
so that his (her) cheerful patience
may reveal your love for us.

We ask this through Christ our Lord.

℞. Amen.

[244]

When the sick person is in great danger.

Lord Jesus Christ,
you took our weakness on yourself
and bore our sufferings in your passion and death.
Hear this prayer for our suffering brother (sister) N.
D **You are his (her) redeemer:**
strengthen his (her) hope for salvation
and in your kindness sustain him (her)
in body and soul.

You live and reign for ever and ever.

℟. **Amen.**

[246]

For those about to die.

Lord God, loving Father,
you are the source of all goodness and love,
and you never refuse forgiveness
to those who are sorry for their sins.
Have mercy on your son (daughter) N.,
who is about to return to you.
E **May this holy anointing**
and our prayer made in faith assist him (her):
relieve his (her) pain, in body and soul,
forgive all his (her) sins,
and strengthen him (her) with your loving pro-
tection.
We ask this, Father, through your son Jesus Christ,
who conquered death
and opened for us the way to eternal life,
and who lives and reigns for ever and ever.

℟. **Amen.**

Lord's Prayer

78. The priest introduces the Lord's Prayer in these or similar words:

**Now let us pray to God as our Lord Jesus Christ
taught us.**

All continue:

**Our Father, who art in heaven,
hallowed be thy name;
thy kingdom come;
thy will be done on earth as it is in heaven.
Give us this day our daily bread;
and forgive us our trespasses
as we forgive those who trespass against us;
and lead us not into temptation,
but deliver us from evil.**

Communion

If the sick person is to receive communion, this takes place after the Lord's Prayer and according to the rite of communion of the sick (nos. 55-58):

The priest shows the holy eucharist to those present, saying:

**This is the Lamb of God
who takes away the sins of the world.
Happy are those who are called to his supper.**

The sick person and all who are to receive communion say once:

Lord, I am not worthy to receive you,
but only say the word and I shall be healed.

The priest goes to the sick person and, showing him the sacrament, says:

The body of Christ (or: **The blood of Christ**).

The sick person answers: **Amen**, and receives communion.

Others present then receive communion in the usual manner.

After communion the minister washes the vessel as usual. Then a period of sacred silence may be observed.

The priest says the concluding prayer:

Let us pray.

A **God our Father, almighty and eternal,**
we confidently call upon you,
that the body [and blood] of Christ
which our brother (sister) has received
may bring him (her)
lasting health in mind and body.

We ask this through Christ our Lord.

℟. **Amen.**

[234]

Father,
you brought to completion
the work of our redemption
through the paschal mystery of Christ your Son.
May we who faithfully proclaim
B his death and resurrection
in these sacramental signs
experience the constant growth of your salvation
    in our lives.

We ask this through Christ our Lord.

℞. Amen.

God our Father,   [235]
you give us a share in the one bread and the one
    cup,
and make us one in Christ.
C May our lives bring your salvation and joy
to all the world.

We ask this through Christ our Lord.

℞. Amen.

Lord,   [236]
in the eucharist we share today
you renew our life.
D Through your Spirit,
make your life grow strong within us
and keep us faithful to you.

We ask this in the name of Jesus our Lord.

℞. Amen.

The priest then blesses the sick person and the others present, either by making the sign of the cross over them with the pyx, if any of the sacrament remains, or by using one of the forms of blessing below.

Blessing

79. The rite concludes with the blessing of the priest.

May God the Father bless you.

℟. **Amen.**

May God the Son heal you.

℟. **Amen.**

May God the Holy Spirit enlighten you.

℟. **Amen.**

A **May God protect you from harm
and grant you salvation.**

℟. **Amen.**

**May he shine on your heart
and lead you to eternal life.**

℟. **Amen.**

**[And may almighty God,
the Father, and the Son, ✝ and the Holy Spirit,
bless you all.**

℟. **Amen.]**

[237]

May the **Lord Jesus Christ be with you to protect you.**

℟. **Amen.**

May he **go before you to guide you and stand behind you to strengthen you.**

℟. **Amen.**

May he **look upon you to keep and bless you.**

℟. **Amen.**

[And may almighty God,
the Father, and the Son, ✝ and the Holy Spirit,
bless you all.

℟. **Amen.]**

RITE OF ANOINTING DURING MASS

80. When the condition of the sick person permits and especially when holy communion is to be received, the anointing may be celebrated during Mass, in the church or, with the consent of the ordinary, in a suitable place in the home of the sick person or the hospital.

81. When anointing is to be administered during Mass, white vestments are used, and the Mass for the sick is celebrated. On the Sundays of Advent, Lent, and the Easter season, on solemnities, Ash Wednesday, and the days of Holy Week, the Mass of the day is celebrated, but the special form for the final blessing is used (nos. 79, 237).

The readings for Mass are taken from the *Lectionary for Mass* (nos. 871-875) or from the rite of anointing (nos. 153-229), unless the priest believes that it would be better for the sick person and those present to choose other readings.

When the Mass for the sick is prohibited, one of the readings may be taken from the texts indicated above, except during the Easter triduum, on Christmas, Epiphany, Ascension, Pentecost, Corpus Christi, or a solemnity which is a holy day of obligation.

82. Anointing is administered after the gospel and homily:

a) In the homily the celebrant should show how the sacred text speaks of the meaning of illness in the history of salvation and of the grace given by the sacrament of anointing. He should also take into consideration the condition of the sick person and other personal circumstances.

b) The celebration of anointing begins with the litany (no. 73) or, if the litany or general intercessions follow the anointing, with the laying on of hands (no. 74). This is followed by the blessing of oil, if it is to take place in accord with no. 21, or by the prayer of thanksgiving over the oil (no. 75) and the anointing itself (no. 76).

c) Unless the litany has preceded the anointing, the general intercessions are then said, concluding with the prayer after anointing (nos. 77, 234-246). The Mass then continues with the presentation of the gifts. The sick person and all present may receive communion under both kinds.

CELEBRATION OF ANOINTING
IN A LARGE CONGREGATION

83.   The rite described below may be used for pilgrimages or other large gatherings of a diocese, city, parish, or society for the sick.

If desired, the same rite may also be used, on occasion, in hospitals.

If, according to the judgment of the ordinary, many sick are to be anointed at the same time, either he or his delegate should see to it that all the disciplinary norms concerning anointing (nos. 8-9) as well as norms concerning pastoral preparation and liturgical celebration (nos. 17, 84, 85) are observed.

If necessary, it is for the ordinary to designate the priests who will take part in the administration of the sacrament.

84. The communal celebration of the anointing of the sick should take place in a church or in some other suitable place, where the sick and others can easily gather.

85. Suitable pastoral preparation should be given beforehand to the sick who are to receive the sacrament, to any other sick persons who may be present, and to those in good health.

The full participation of those present should be encouraged by the use of appropriate songs to foster common prayer and manifest the Easter joy proper to this sacrament.

Celebration outside Mass

86. It is preferable that sick persons who are to be anointed and wish to confess their sins receive the sacrament of penance before the celebration of anointing.

87. The rite begins with the reception of the sick. The priest should manifest to them the concern of Christ for human illness and for the role of the sick in the people of God.

88.   The penitential rite may then be celebrated if desired (no. 71).

89.   The celebration of the word of God follows. It may consist of one or more readings from scripture, together with song. Readings may be taken from the lectionary for the sick (nos. 153-229) or, if the sick persons and others present would be better served by different readings, others may be chosen. A brief period of silence may follow the homily.

90.   The celebration of the sacrament begins with the litany (no. 73) or with the laying on of hands (no. 74). After the prayer of anointing has been heard at least once by those present, suitable songs may be sung while the sick are being anointed. The general intercessions, if they follow the anointing, are concluded with the prayer after anointing (no. 77) or with the Lord's Prayer which may be sung by all.

If there are several priests present, each one lays hands on some of the sick and anoints them, using the sacramental form. The principal celebrant recites the prayers.

91.   Before the rite of dismissal the blessing is given (nos. 79 and 237), and the celebration may conclude with an appropriate song.

Celebration during Mass

92.   The reception of the sick takes place at the beginning of Mass after the greeting and introductory words.

The liturgy of the word and the rite of anointing are celebrated as indicated in nos. 89-91.

CHAPTER III

VIATICUM

93. The pastor and other priests who are entrusted with the spiritual care of the sick should do everything they can to insure that those in danger of death receive the body and blood of Christ in viaticum. A time should be chosen when the necessary pastoral preparation can be given to the sick person and also to his family and those who take care of him; the circumstances and individuals involved should be taken into consideration.

94. Viaticum may be given during Mass, if the ordinary allows the celebration of the eucharist for that purpose (no. 26), or outside Mass, according to the rites and norms below.

95. Those who are unable to receive under the form of bread may receive the eucharist under the form of wine alone.

If Mass is not celebrated in the presence of the sick person, the blood of the Lord should be kept in a properly covered chalice which is placed in the tabernacle after Mass. The precious blood should be carried in a vessel which is closed in such a way as to eliminate all danger of spilling. The priest should choose the manner of giving communion under both kinds which is suitable in the individual case. If some of the precious blood remains, it should be consumed by the minister; he will also wash the vessel.

96. All who take part in the celebration may receive communion under both kinds.

VIATICUM DURING MASS

97. When viaticum is administered during Mass, the Mass of the Holy Eucharist or the Mass for Viaticum may be celebrated. White vestments are used. On the Sundays of Advent, Lent, and the Easter season, on solemnities, Ash Wednesday, and the days of Holy Week, the Mass of the day is celebrated. Either the special form of the final blessing (nos. 79, 237) or the usual blessing at the end of Mass may be used.

The readings may be taken from the *Lectionary for Mass* (nos. 904-909) or from nos. 247-258 or 153-229. If the sick and the others present would be better served by different readings, others may be chosen.

When a votive Mass is prohibited, one of the readings may be taken from the texts indicated above, except during the Easter triduum and on Christmas, Epiphany, Ascension, Pentecost, Corpus Christi, or a solemnity which is a holy day of obligation.

98. If necessary, the priest should hear the sacramental confession of the sick person before the celebration of Mass.

99. Mass is celebrated in the usual way. The priest should note the following:

a) According to circumstances, a short homily on the sacred text should be given after the gospel. It should take into account the condition of the sick person and explain the importance and meaning of viaticum (see nos. 26-28) to the sick person and to the others present.

b) If the sick person is to renew his baptismal profession of faith (no. 108), the priest should introduce this at the conclusion of the homily. This renewal takes the place of the usual profession of faith in the Mass.

c) The general intercessions may be adapted to the particular celebration or may be taken from no. 109. The general intercessions may be omitted if the sick person has made the profession of faith and it appears that they will tire him too much.

d) The priest and those present may give the sick person the sign of peace at the appointed time during Mass.

e) The sick person and all present may receive communion under both kinds. When the priest gives communion to the sick person, he uses the form for viaticum (no. 112).

f) At the end of Mass the priest may use the special form of blessing (nos. 79, 237) and may also add the form for the plenary indulgence for the dying (no. 106).

VIATICUM OUTSIDE MASS

100. The priest should inquire whether the sick person wishes to confess and, if possible, he should hear his confession before the administration of viaticum. If the sacramental confession is made during the celebration, it takes place at the beginning of the rite. If the confession of the sick person does not take place during the rite or if there are others to receive communion, the penitential rite should be celebrated.

Introductory Rites

101. Wearing the appropriate vestments, the priest approaches the sick person and greets him and the others present in a friendly manner. He may use this greeting:

A Peace to this house and to all who live in it.

B The peace of the Lord be with you.

[230]

C The grace of our Lord Jesus Christ and the love of God and the fellowship of the Holy Spirit be with you all.

℟. And also with you.

[231]

The grace and peace of God our Father and the Lord Jesus Christ be with you.

℟. Blessed be God the Father of our Lord Jesus Christ.

Or:

℟. And also with you.

Then he places the sacrament on the table, and all adore it.

102. According to the circumstances, the priest may sprinkle the sick person and the room with holy water, saying the following words or those given in a particular ritual:

Let this water call to mind
your baptismal sharing
in Christ's redeeming passion and resurrection.

103. Afterwards the priest addresses those present, using the following instruction or one better suited to the sick person's condition:

My brothers and sisters:

Before he left this world to return to the Father, our Lord Jesus Christ gave us this sacrament of his body and blood, so that when the hour comes for us to pass from this life to join him, we may be reassured and strengthened by this pledge of our

own resurrection, this food for our journey, the Lord's own body and blood. Now let us pray for our brother (sister), one with him (her) in Christian love.

Penitential Rite

104. If necessary, the priest then hears the person's sacramental confession. This may be, in case of necessity, a generic confession.

105. When sacramental confession is not part of the rite or if there are others to receive communion, the priest invites the sick person and all present to join in the penitential rite:

My brothers and sisters, to prepare ourselves for this celebration, let us call to mind our sins.

After a brief silence, all say:

**I confess to almighty God,
and to you, my brothers and sisters,
that I have sinned through my own fault**

They strike their breast:

A **in my thoughts and in my words,
in what I have done,
and in what I have failed to do;
and I ask blessed Mary, ever Virgin,
all the angels and saints,
and you, my brothers and sisters,
to pray for me to the Lord our God.**

The priest concludes:

A **May almighty God have mercy on us,**
forgive us our sins,
and bring us to everlasting life.

All answer: **Amen.**

[232]

After a brief silence, the priest says:

Lord, we have sinned against you:
Lord, have mercy.

All answer: **Lord, have mercy.**

B Priest: **Lord, show us your mercy and love.**

All answer: **And grant us your salvation.**

The priest concludes:

May almighty God have mercy on us,
forgive us our sins,
and bring us to everlasting life.

All answer: **Amen.**

[233]

After a brief silence, the priest or one of the others present says the following or other invocations with the Kyrie:

C **You brought us to salvation by your paschal mystery:**
Lord, have mercy.

All answer: **Lord, have mercy.**

Priest: **You renew us by the wonders of your passion:**
Christ, have mercy.

All answer: **Christ, have mercy.**

Priest: **You make us sharers in your paschal sacrifice by our partaking of your body:**

C **Lord, have mercy.**

All answer: **Lord, have mercy.**

The priest concludes:

May almighty God have mercy on us,
forgive us our sins,
and bring us to everlasting life.

All answer: **Amen.**

Indulgence

106. At the conclusion of the sacrament of penance or the penitential rite the priest may give the plenary indulgence for the dying:

A **By the power the Apostolic See has given me,**
I grant you a plenary indulgence
and pardon for all your sins,
in the name of the Father, and of the Son,
✝ and of the Holy Spirit.

℟. **Amen.**

B **Through the suffering, death, and resurrection of Jesus Christ,**

B
may almighty God free you from all punishments
in this life and in the life to come.
May he open paradise to you
and welcome you to the joy of eternal life.

℟. Amen.

Reading from Scripture

107. It is most fitting that one of those present
or the priest read a brief text from scripture, for
example:

John 6:54-55 or John 6:54-59

A
"He who eats my flesh
and drinks my blood
has eternal life,
and I will raise him up at the last day.
For my flesh is food indeed,
and my blood is drink indeed.
[He who eats my flesh
and drinks my blood
abides in me, and I in him.
As the living Father sent me,
and I live because of the Father,
so he who eats me
will live because of me.
This is the bread which came down from heaven,
not such as the fathers ate and died;
he who eats this bread will live for ever."
This he said in the synagogue as he taught at
    Capernaum.]

John 14:6

Jesus said,
B **"I am the way, and the truth, and the life;**
no one comes to the Father, but by me."

John 14:23

Jesus answered,
"If a man loves me, he will keep my word,
C **and my Father will love him,**
and we will come to him
and make our home with him."

John 15:4

"Abide in me, and I in you.
D **As the branch cannot bear fruit by itself,**
unless it abides in the vine,
neither can you, unless you abide in me."

1 Corinthians 11:26

E **For as often as you eat this bread and drink the**
cup, you proclaim the Lord's death until he comes.

Other suitable texts may be selected from nos. 247-258 or 153-229. Depending on circumstances, the priest may give a brief explanation of the text.

Baptismal Profession of Faith

108. It is desirable that the sick person renew his baptismal profession of faith before he receives viaticum. The priest gives a brief introduction and then asks the following questions:

Do you believe in God, the Father almighty, creator of heaven and earth?

℟. **I do.**

Do you believe in Jesus Christ, his only Son, our Lord, who was born of the Virgin Mary, was cruci-fied, died, and was buried, rose from the dead, and is now seated at the right hand of the Father?

℟. **I do.**

Do you believe in the Holy Spirit, the holy catholic Church, the communion of saints, the forgiveness of sins, the resurrection of the body, and life ever-lasting?

℟. **I do.**

Litany

109.   If the condition of the sick person permits, a brief litany is recited in these or similar words. The sick person, if he is able, and all present re-spond:

**My brothers and sisters,
with one heart let us pray
to the Lord Jesus Christ.**

**You loved us, Lord,
to the very end of your life,
and you willingly accepted death
that we might have life:
listen to our prayer for our brother (sister).**

℟. **Lord, hear our prayer.**

You told us:
"He who eats my flesh and drinks
my blood has eternal life":
listen to our prayer for our brother (sister).

℟. Lord, hear our prayer.

You invited us to join in that banquet
where pain and sorrow,
death and separation will be no more:
listen to our prayer for our brother (sister).

℟. Lord, hear our prayer.

Viaticum

110. The priest introduces the Lord's Prayer in these or similar words:

Now let us pray to God as our Lord Jesus Christ
　taught us.

All continue:

Our Father, who art in heaven,
hallowed be thy name;
thy kingdom come;
thy will be done on earth as it is in heaven.
Give us this day our daily bread;
and forgive us our trespasses
as we forgive those who trespass against us;
and lead us not into temptation,
but deliver us from evil.

111. Then the priest shows the holy eucharist to those present, saying:

**This is the Lamb of God
who takes away the sins of the world.
Happy are those who are called to his supper.**

The sick person and all who are to receive communion say once:

**Lord, I am not worthy to receive you,
but only say the word and I shall be healed.**

112. The priest goes to the sick person and, showing him the sacrament, says:

The body of Christ (or: **The blood of Christ**).

The sick person answers: **Amen.**

Immediately, or after giving communion, the priest adds:

**May the Lord Jesus Christ protect you and lead
you to eternal life.**

The sick person answers: **Amen.**

Others present then receive communion in the usual manner.

113. After communion the priest washes the vessel as usual. Then a period of sacred silence may be observed.

Concluding Rite

114. The priest says the concluding prayer:

Let us pray.

A

Father,
your Son, Jesus Christ, is our way, our truth, and
    our life.
Our brother (sister) N., entrusts himself (herself)
    to you
with full confidence in all your promises.
Refresh him (her) with the body and blood of your
    Son
and lead him (her) to your kingdom in peace.

We ask this through Christ our Lord.

℟. Amen.

[259]

B

Lord,
you are the source of eternal health
for those who believe in you.
May our brother (sister) N.,
who has been refreshed with food and drink from
    heaven,
safely reach your kingdom of light and life.

We ask this through Christ our Lord.

℟. Amen.

[57]

C

God our Father, almighty and eternal,
we confidently call upon you,
that the body [and blood] of Christ
which our brother (sister) has received
may bring him (her)
lasting health in mind and body.

C **We ask this through Christ our Lord.**

℟. **Amen.**

He then blesses the sick person and those present:

A **May almighty God bless you,
the Father, and the Son, ✝ and the Holy Spirit.**

℟. **Amen.**

The form of blessing in nos. 79, 237-238 may be used or, if any of the sacrament remains, the priest may bless the sick person with it by making the sign of the cross over him.

[79]

May God the Father bless you.

℟. **Amen.**

May God the Son heal you.

℟. **Amen.**

May God the Holy Spirit enlighten you.

B ℟. **Amen.**

**May God protect you from harm
and grant you salvation.**

℟. **Amen.**

**May he shine on your heart
and lead you to eternal life.**

℟. **Amen.**

B [And may almighty God,
the Father, and the Son, ✝ and the Holy Spirit,
bless you all.

℞. Amen.]

[237]

May the Lord Jesus Christ be with you to protect
  you.

℞. Amen.

May he go before you to guide you and stand behind you to give you strength.

C ℞. Amen.

May he look upon you, to keep you and bless you.

℞. Amen.

[And may almighty God,
the Father, and the Son, ✝ and the Holy Spirit,
bless you all.

℞. Amen.]

[238]

D May the blessing of almighty God,
the Father, and the Son, ✝ and the Holy Spirit,
come upon you and remain with you for ever.

℞. Amen.

Sign of Peace

The priest and the others present may then give
the sick person the sign of peace.

CHAPTER IV

RITE OF THE SACRAMENTS
FOR THOSE NEAR DEATH

CONTINUOUS RITE OF PENANCE, ANOINTING, AND VIATICUM

115. The priest should inquire whether the sick person wishes to confess and, if possible, he should hear his confession before the administration of anointing and viaticum. If the sacramental confession is made during the celebration, it takes place at the beginning of the rite, before the anointing. Otherwise, the penitential rite should be celebrated.

116. In cases where the sick person is in imminent danger of dying, he should be anointed immediately with a single anointing and then given viaticum. In more urgent cases, according to the norm of no. 30, he should be given viaticum immediately, without the anointing, so that in his passage from this life, he may be strengthened by the body of Christ, the pledge of the resurrection. The faithful in the danger of death are obliged by the precept of receiving holy communion.

117. If possible, confirmation in the danger of death and anointing of the sick should not be celebrated in a continuous rite, lest the two anointings create confusion between the two sacraments. If necessary, however, confirmation is celebrated immediately before the blessing of the oil of the sick; the imposition of hands which is a part of the rite of anointing is then omitted.

Introductory Rites

118. Wearing the appropriate vestments, the priest approaches the sick person and greets him and the others present in a friendly manner. He may use this greeting:

A **Peace to this house and to all who live in it.**

B **The peace of the Lord be with you.**

[230]

C **The grace of our Lord Jesus Christ and the love of God and the fellowship of the Holy Spirit be with you all.**

℟. **And also with you.**

[231]

The grace and peace of God our Father and the Lord Jesus Christ be with you.

D ℟. **Blessed be God the Father of our Lord Jesus Christ.**

Or:

℟. **And also with you.**

Then he places the sacrament on the table, and all adore it.

According to the circumstances, the priest may sprinkle the sick person and the room with holy water, saying the following words or those given in a particular ritual:

Let this water call to mind
your baptismal sharing
in Christ's redeeming passion and resurrection.

119. If necessary, the priest prepares the sick person in a kindly manner for the celebration of the sacraments. Depending on the circumstances, he reads a brief gospel text to move the sick person to penance and the love of God. Or he may use the following instruction or one better adapted to the sick person's condition:

Dear brothers and sisters:

The Lord Jesus is always with us, renewing the life of his people through the power of the sacraments. He forgives the sins of the repentant through the ministry of his priests; he comforts the sick through the sacrament of anointing. To all who await his return, he gives his body and blood as food to sustain them on their journey and to strengthen them in the hope of eternal life. So now let us offer these sacraments to our brother (sister), and assist him (her) with our loving prayers.

Penance

120.   If necessary, the priest then hears the person's sacramental confession. This may be, in case of necessity, a generic confession.

121.   When sacramental confession is not part of the rite or if there are others to receive communion, the priest invites the sick person and all present to join in the penitential rite:

My brothers and sisters, to prepare ourselves for this celebration, let us call to mind our sins.

After a brief silence, all say:

**I confess to almighty God,
and to you, my brothers and sisters,
that I have sinned through my own fault**

They strike their breast:

A   **in my thoughts and in my words,
in what I have done,
and in what I have failed to do;
and I ask blessed Mary, ever Virgin,
all the angels and saints,
and you, my brothers and sisters,
to pray for me to the Lord our God.**

The priest concludes:

**May almighty God have mercy on us,
forgive us our sins,
and bring us to everlasting life.**

All answer: **Amen.**

[232]

After a brief silence, the priest says:

Lord, we have sinned against you:
Lord, have mercy.

All answer: **Lord, have mercy.**

Priest: **Lord, show us your mercy and love.**

All answer: **And grant us your salvation.**

The priest concludes:

May almighty God have mercy on us,
forgive us our sins,
and bring us to everlasting life.

All answer: **Amen.**

[233]

After a brief silence, the priest or one of the others present says the following or other invocations with the Kyrie:

You brought us to salvation by your paschal mystery:
Lord, have mercy.

All answer: **Lord, have mercy.**

Priest: **You renew us by the wonders of your passion:**
Christ, have mercy.

All answer: **Christ, have mercy.**

Priest: **You make us sharers in your paschal sacrifice**
by our partaking of your body:
Lord, have mercy.

All answer: **Lord, have mercy.**

The priest concludes:

May almighty God have mercy on us,
forgive us our sins,
and bring us to everlasting life.

All answer: **Amen.**

Indulgence

122.   At the conclusion of the sacrament of penance or the penitential rite the priest may give the plenary indulgence for the dying:

By the power the Apostolic See has given me,
I grant you a plenary indulgence
and pardon for all your sins,
in the name of the Father, and of the Son,
   ✝ and of the Holy Spirit.

℟. **Amen.**

Through the suffering, death, and resurrection of
   Jesus Christ,
may almighty God free you from all punishments
in this life and in the life to come.
May he open paradise to you
and welcome you to the joy of eternal life.

℟. **Amen.**

Baptismal Profession of Faith

123.   If the condition of the sick person permits, the baptismal profession of faith and a brief litany follow.

[108]

The priest gives a brief introduction and then asks the following questions:

Do you believe in God, the Father almighty, creator of heaven and earth?

℟. **I do.**

Do you believe in Jesus Christ, his only Son our Lord, who was born of the Virgin Mary, was crucified, died, and was buried, rose from the dead, and is now seated at the right hand of the Father?

℟. **I do.**

Do you believe in the Holy Spirit, the holy catholic Church, the communion of saints, the forgiveness of sins, the resurrection of the body, and life everlasting?

℟. **I do.**

Litany

The following may be adapted to express the prayer of the sick person and of those present. The sick person, if he is able, and all present respond.

Let us pray, dear friends, for our brother (sister) N., that the Lord may now strengthen him (her) with his sacraments.

God our Father, see in our brother (sister) the patient suffering of your own Son.

℟. **Lord, hear our prayer.**

Watch over him (her) always and keep him (her) in your love.

℟. **Lord, hear our prayer.**

Give him (her) your strength and your peace.

℟. **Lord, hear our prayer.**

124. If the sacrament of confirmation is celebrated in the same rite, the priest continues as indicated in nos. 136-137. In this case the laying on of hands (no. 125) is omitted, and the priest then blesses the oil, if this is to be done, and performs the anointing (nos. 126-128).

Sacrament of Anointing

125. The priest lays his hands on the head of the sick person in silence.

126. If oil is to be blessed, in accord with no. 21, the priest says:

A **Lord, bless this oil ✝ and bless our sick brother (sister) whom we will anoint with it.**

[242]

B **Praise to you, almighty God and Father.**
You sent your Son to live among us and bring us salvation.

℟. **Blessed be God.**

Praise to you, Lord Jesus Christ, the Father's only
   Son.
You humbled yourself to share in our humanity
   and desired to cure all our illnesses.

℟. Blessed be God.

Praise to you, God the Holy Spirit, the Consoler.
You heal our sickness with your mighty power.

B ℟. Blessed be God.

Lord,
mercifully listen to our prayers
and bless this oil intended to ease the sufferings
   of your people.
May those for whom we pray in faith
and who are anointed with this holy oil,
be freed of the illness that afflicts them.

We ask this through Christ our Lord.

℟. Amen.

[75]

Let us pray.

Lord God, loving Father,
you bring healing to the sick
C through your Son Jesus Christ.
Hear us as we pray to you in faith,
and send the Holy Spirit, man's Helper and Friend,
upon this oil, which nature has provided
to serve the needs of men.
May your blessing ✝

come upon all who are anointed with this oil,
that they may be freed from pain and illness
and made well again in body, mind, and soul.

C Father, may this oil be blessed for our use
in the name of our Lord Jesus Christ
who lives and reigns with you for ever and ever.

℟. **Amen.**

Prayer of Thanksgiving

127. If the oil is already blessed, the priest may
say the prayer of thanksgiving over the oil:

**Praise to you, almighty God and Father.
You sent your Son to live among us and bring us
    salvation.**

℟. **Blessed be God.**

**Praise to you, Lord Jesus Christ, the Father's only
    Son.
You humbled yourself to share in our humanity,
    and you desired to cure all our illnesses.**

℟. **Blessed be God.**

**Praise to you, God the Holy Spirit, the Consoler.
You heal our sickness with your mighty power.**

℟. **Blessed be God.**

**Lord God,
with faith in you
our brother (sister) will be anointed with this holy
    oil.**

Ease his (her) sufferings and strengthen him (her) in his (her) weakness.

We ask this through Christ our Lord.

℟. **Amen.**

Anointing

128.   Then the priest takes the oil and anoints the sick person on the forehead and the hands, saying once:

**Through this holy anointing
may the Lord in his love and mercy help you
with the grace of the Holy Spirit.**

℟. **Amen.**

**May the Lord who frees you from sin
save you and raise you up.**

℟. **Amen.**

Lord's Prayer

129.   The priest introduces the Lord's Prayer in these or similar words:

Now let us pray to God as our Lord Jesus Christ taught us.

All continue:

**Our Father, who art in heaven,
hallowed be thy name;
thy kingdom come;
thy will be done on earth as it is in heaven.**

Give us this day our daily bread;
and forgive us our trespasses
as we forgive those who trespass against us;
and lead us not into temptation,
but deliver us from evil.

Viaticum

130. Then the priest shows the holy eucharist to those present, saying:

**This is the Lamb of God
who takes away the sins of the world.
Happy are those who are called to his supper.**

The sick person and all who are to receive communion say once:

**Lord, I am not worthy to receive you,
but only say the word and I shall be healed.**

131. The priest goes to the sick person and, showing him the sacrament, says:

The body of Christ (or: **The blood of Christ**).

The sick person answers: **Amen.**

Immediately, or after giving communion, the priest adds:

May the Lord Jesus Christ protect you and lead you to eternal life.

The sick person then answers: **Amen.**

Others present then receive communion in the usual manner.

132. After communion the priest washes the vessel as usual. Then a period of sacred silence may be observed.

Concluding Rite

133. The priest says the concluding prayer:

Let us pray.

Father,
your Son, Jesus Christ,
is our way, our truth, and our life.
Our brother (sister) N., entrusts himself (herself)
**   to you**
with full confidence in all your promises.
Refresh him (her) with the body and blood
**   of your Son**
and lead him (her) to your kingdom in peace.

We ask this through Christ our Lord.

℟. **Amen.**

[259]

Lord,
you are the source of eternal health
for those who believe in you.
May our brother (sister) N.,
who has been refreshed with food and drink from
**   heaven,**
safely reach your kingdom of light and life.

We ask this through Christ our Lord.

℟. **Amen.**

[57]

God our Father, almighty and eternal,
we confidently call upon you,
that the body [and blood] of Christ
which our brother (sister) has received
C may bring him (her)
lasting health in mind and body.

We ask this through Christ our Lord.

R℣. Amen.

Blessing

He then blesses the sick person and those
present:

May almighty God bless you,
A the Father, and the Son, ✝ and the Holy Spirit.

R℣. Amen.

[79]

May God the Father bless you.

R℣. Amen.

May God the Son heal you.

R℣. Amen.

B May God the Holy Spirit enlighten you.

R℣. Amen.

May God protect you from harm,
and grant you salvation.

R℣. Amen.

**May he shine on your heart
and lead you to eternal life.**

B ℞. **Amen.**

**[And may almighty God,
the Father, and the Son, ✝ and the Holy Spirit,
bless you all.**

℞. **Amen.]**

[237]

**May the Lord Jesus Christ be with you to protect
you.**

℞. **Amen.**

**May he go before you to guide you and stand be-
hind you to give you strength.**

C ℞. **Amen.**

May he look upon you, to keep you and bless you.

℞. **Amen.**

**[And may almighty God,
the Father, and the Son, ✝ and the Holy Spirit,
bless you all.**

℞. **Amen.]**

Sign of Peace

The priest and the others present may then give
the sick person the sign of peace.

RITE OF ANOINTING WITHOUT VIATICUM

134. If a sick person who is near death is to be anointed but not given viaticum, the rite in nos. 119-129 is used with the following changes:

a) The initial instruction (no. 119) is adapted in this manner:

My brothers and sisters:

Our Lord Jesus Christ has told us through his apostle James: "Is there anyone sick among you? Let him call for the elders of the Church, and let them pray over him and anoint him in the name of the Lord. This prayer, made in faith, will save the sick man. The Lord will restore his health, and if he has committed any sins, they will be forgiven."

Let us entrust our sick brother (sister) to the power and strength of Jesus Christ, that Christ may ease his (her) sufferings and grant him (her) health and salvation.

b) After the anointing, the priest says a prayer corresponding to the sick person's condition:

[243]

When the illness is the result of advanced age.

A **Lord,
look kindly on our brother (sister)
who has grown weak under the burden of his (her)
    years.**

In this holy anointing
he (she) asks for the grace of health in body and
    soul.
By the power of your Holy Spirit,
A make him (her) firm in faith and sure in hope,
so that his (her) cheerful patience
may reveal your love for us.

We ask this through Christ our Lord.

℞. **Amen.**

[244]

When the sick person is in great danger.

Lord Jesus Christ,
you took our weakness on yourself
and bore our sufferings in your passion and death.
Hear this prayer for our suffering brother (sister) N.
B You are his (her) Redeemer:
strengthen his (her) hope for salvation
and in your kindness sustain him (her)
in body and soul.

You live and reign for ever and ever.

℞. **Amen.**

For those about to die.   [246]

Lord God, loving Father,
you are the source of all goodness and love,
C and you never refuse forgiveness
to those who are sorry for their sins.
Have mercy on your son (daughter) N.,
who is about to return to you.

May this holy anointing
and our prayer made in faith assist him (her):
relieve his (her) pain, in body and soul,
forgive all his (her) sins,
and strengthen him (her) with your loving protection.

We ask this, Father, through your Son Jesus Christ,
who conquered death
and opened for us the way to eternal life,
and who lives and reigns for ever and ever.

℞. Amen.

CONDITIONAL ANOINTING

135. If the priest doubts whether a sick person is still living, he may anoint him in this manner:

He goes to the sick person and, if time allows, first says:

Let us pray with faith for our brother (sister) N.
May the Lord come to him (her)
  with his mercy and love,
and renew his (her) strength
  through this holy anointing.

℟. **Lord, hear our prayer.**

He immediately anoints him (her), saying this form:

If you are alive, we pray:
through this holy anointing
may the Lord in his love and mercy help you
with the grace of the Holy Spirit.

℟. **Amen.**

May the Lord who frees you from sin
save you and raise you up.

℟. **Amen.**

The priest may add a prayer corresponding to the condition of the sick person:

[244]

When the sick person is in great danger.

A

Lord Jesus Christ,
you took our weakness on yourself
and bore our sufferings in your passion and death.
Hear this prayer for our suffering brother (sister) N.
You are his (her) Redeemer:
strengthen his (her) hope for salvation
and in your kindness sustain him (her)
in body and soul.

You live and reign for ever and ever.

℟. **Amen.**

[246]

For those about to die.

B

Lord God, loving Father,
you are the source of all goodness and love,
and you never refuse forgiveness
to those who are sorry for their sins.
Have mercy on your son (daughter) N.,
who is about to return to you.
May this holy anointing
and our prayer made in faith assist him (her):
relieve his (her) pain, in body and soul,
forgive all his (her) sins,
and strengthen him (her) with your loving protec-
    tion.

We ask this, Father, through your Son Jesus Christ,
who conquered death
and opened for us the way to eternal life,
and who lives and reigns for ever and ever.

℟. **Amen.**

CHAPTER V

CONFIRMATION OF A PERSON
IN DANGER OF DEATH

136. Whenever the circumstances permit, the entire rite is to be used. In the case of urgent necessity, the rite is as follows:

The priest lays hands upon the sick person as he says:

**All-powerful God, Father of our Lord Jesus Christ,
by water and the Holy Spirit
you freed your son (daughter) from sin
and gave him (her) new life.
Send your Holy Spirit upon him (her)
to be his (her) Helper and Guide.
Give him (her) the spirit of wisdom and understanding,
the spirit of right judgment and courage,
the spirit of knowledge and reverence.
Fill him (her) with the spirit of wonder and awe in
  your presence.**

We ask this through Christ our Lord.

℟. **Amen.**

Then he dips his right thumb in the chrism and makes the sign of the cross on the forehead of the one to be confirmed, as he says:

**N., receive the seal of the Holy Spirit,
the Gift of the Father.**

The newly confirmed answers, if he (she) is able:

Amen.

Other parts of the preparatory and concluding rites in the rite of confirmation may be added in individual cases, depending on the circumstances.

137.   In the case of extreme necessity, it is sufficient for the priest to sign the sick person with the chrism while saying the sacramental form:

**N., receive the seal of the Holy Spirit,
the Gift of the Father.**

CHAPTER VI

RITE FOR THE COMMENDATION
OF THE DYING

138. Charity towards one's neighbor urges Christians to express fellowship with a dying brother or sister by praying with him or her for God's mercy and for confidence in Christ.

139. Prayers, litanies, aspirations, psalms, and readings from scripture are provided in this chapter for the commendation of souls. Thus the dying person, if still conscious, may imitate Christ in the face of the anxiety about death that is common to all men and may accept suffering and death in the hope of heavenly life and resurrection, for Christ, by his power, destroyed our death by his own dying.

Those who are present may also draw consolation from these prayers even if the dying person is not conscious and so come to a better understanding of the paschal character of Christian death. This may be visibly expressed by making the sign of the cross on the forehead of the dying person, who was first signed with the cross of baptism.

140. Prayers and readings may be chosen freely from those which follow, and others may be added if the situation demands. They should always be adapted to the spiritual and physical condition of the person as well as to other circumstances. They should be recited in a slow, quiet voice, alternated with periods of silence. Often it may be desirable to recite one or more of the brief formulas given below with the dying person and, if necessary, they may be softly repeated two or three times.

141. Immediately after death has occurred, all may kneel and one of those present or a priest or deacon, if present, recites the prayer in no. 151.

142. It is the responsibility of priests and deacons, whenever possible, to assist the dying person and those who are with him and to recite the prayers of commendation and the prayer after death. The presence of these ministers clearly shows the Christian the meaning of death in the fellowship of the Church. When a priest or deacon is unable to be present because of other serious pastoral obligations, he should instruct the laity to assist the dying by reciting the prayers contained in this chapter or other prayers; texts of these prayers and readings should be made readily available to them.

143.   Short Texts

(Romans 8:35)

What can come between us and the love of Christ?

(Romans 14:8)

Whether we live or die we are the Lord's.

(2 Corinthians 5:1)

We have an everlasting home in heaven.

(1 Thessalonians 4:17)

We shall be with the Lord for ever.

(1 John 3:2)

We shall see God as he really is.

(1 John 3:14)

We have passed from death to life because we love the brothers.

(Psalm 24:1)

To you I lift up my soul.

(Psalm 26:1)

The Lord is my light and my salvation.

(Psalm 26:13)

I believe that I shall see the goodness of the Lord in the land of the living.

(Psalm 41:3)

My soul thirsts for the living God.

(Psalm 22:4)

Though I walk in the shadow of death, I will fear no evil for you are with me.

(Matthew 25:34)

Come, blessed of my Father, says the Lord Jesus, and take possession of the kingdom prepared for you.

(Luke 23:43)

Truly I say to you: Today you will be with me in paradise, says the Lord Jesus.

(John 14:2)

In my Father's home there are many dwelling places, says the Lord Jesus.

(John 14:2-3)

The Lord Jesus says, I go to prepare you a place, and I will take you with me.

(John 17:24)

I wish that where I am, they also may be with me, says the Lord Jesus.

(John 6:40)

All who believe in the Son will have eternal life.

(Psalm 30:6a)

Into your hands, Lord, I commit my spirit.

(Acts 7:59)

Lord Jesus, receive my spirit.

Holy Mary, pray for me.

St. Joseph, pray for me.

Jesus, Mary, and Joseph, assist me in my last agony.

144.   Biblical Readings

Some of the readings from scripture may be chosen from those given in nos. 153-229 or from the following:

Readings from the Old Testament: Isaiah 35:3-4, 6c-7, 10; Job 19:23-27a.

Psalms: 22; 24:1, 4b-11; 90; 113:1-8; 114:3-5; 120: 1-4; 122.

Readings from the New Testament: 1 Corinthians 15:1-4; 1 John 4:16; Revelation 21:1-5a, 6-7.

Gospels: Matthew 25:1-13; Mark 15:33-37; Mark 16:1-8; Luke 22:39-46; Luke 23:42-43; Luke 24: 1-8; John 6:37-40; John 14:1-6, 23, 27.

145. If the dying person is not able to bear lengthy prayers, it is recommended that, according to the particular circumstances, those present pray for him by reciting the litany of the saints, or at least some invocations from it, with the response "pray for him (her)." Special mention may be made of the patron saint or saints of the dying person or his family. Those present may also recite other customary prayers.

When the moment of death seems to be near, someone may say some of the following prayers which are in accord with the Christian disposition for death.

146. Prayers

In the name of God the almighty Father who created you,
in the name of Jesus Christ, Son of the living God, who suffered for you,

in the name of the Holy Spirit who was poured out
   upon you,
go forth, faithful Christian.
May you live in peace this day,
may your home be with God in Zion,
with Mary the virgin Mother of God,
with Joseph, and all the angels and saints.

147.
My brother (sister) in faith,
I entrust you to God who created you.
May you return to the one
who formed you from the dust of this earth.
May Mary, the angels, and all the saints
come to meet you as you go forth from this life.
May Christ who was crucified for you
bring you freedom and peace.
May Christ, the Son of God, who died for you
take you into his kingdom.
May Christ, the Good Shepherd,
give you a place within his flock.
May he forgive your sins
and keep you among his people.
May you see your Redeemer face to face
and enjoy the sight of God for ever.

℟. Amen.

148.
Accept your servant, Lord,
into the place of salvation for which he (she)
   hopes.

℟. Amen.

**Free your servant, Lord,
from every pain and suffering.**

℞. **Amen.**

**Free your servant, Lord,
as you freed Noah from the flood.**

℞. **Amen.**

**Free your servant, Lord,
as you freed Abraham from his enemies.**

℞. **Amen.**

**Free your servant, Lord,
as you freed Job from his sufferings.**

℞. **Amen.**

**Free your servant, Lord,
as you freed Moses from the hand of the Pharaoh.**

℞. **Amen.**

**Free your servant, Lord,
as you freed Daniel from the den of lions.**

℞. **Amen.**

**Free your servant, Lord,
as you freed the three young men from the burning
   fire.**

℞. **Amen.**

**Free your servant, Lord,
as you freed Susanna from false witness.**

℞. **Amen.**

Free your servant, Lord,
as you freed David from the attacks of Saul and
   Goliath.

R̝. Amen.

Free your servant, Lord,
as you freed Peter and Paul from prison.

R̝. Amen.

Free your servant, Lord,
through Jesus our Savior,
who suffered death for us
and gave us eternal life.

R̝. Amen.

149.
Lord, Jesus Christ, Savior of the world,
we commend your servant N. to you and pray
   for him (her).
In mercy you came to earth for his (her) sake:
accept him (her) into the joy of your kingdom.
Though he (she) has failed and sinned,
he (she) has not denied the Father, the Son,
   and the Holy Spirit,
but has believed and has worshiped God the
   Creator:
accept him (her) into the joy of your kingdom.

R̝. Amen.

150.   The following antiphon may be said or
sung.

A
Hail, holy Queen, mother of mercy,
our life, our sweetness, and our hope.
To you do we cry,
poor banished children of Eve.
To you do we send up our sighs,
mourning and weeping in this vale of tears.
Turn then, most gracious advocate,
your eyes of mercy toward us,
and after this exile
show to us the blessed fruit of your womb, Jesus.
O clement, O loving,
O sweet Virgin Mary.

B
O Mary, our Queen,
Virgin-Mother compassionate,
source of our comfort, hope of life immortal.

We are Eve's children,
who seek a new mother.
We call your name with love,
we, God's holy people,
exiled to this tearful valley.

Look down with love,
from your place in heaven:
plead for us now,
as once you shared with us life's pain,
its fear, its sorrow.

Christ Jesus, Lord and Savior,
was the Child you bore for us:
one day bring us to him for ever.

O holy, O loving, O gentle
blest virgin, Mary.

151. Immediately after death, the following should be said:

Saints of God, come to his (her) aid!
Come to meet him (her), angels of the Lord!

℟. **Receive his (her) soul and present him (her) to God the Most High.**

May Christ, who called you, take you to himself;
may angels lead you to Abraham's side.

℟. **Receive . . .**

Give him (her) eternal rest, O Lord,
and may your light shine on him (her) for ever.

℟. **Receive . . .**

Let us pray.

We commend our brother (sister) N. to you, Lord.
Now that he (she) has passed from this life,
may he (she) live on in your presence.
In your mercy and love,
forgive whatever sins he (she) may have committed
through human weakness.

We ask this through Christ our Lord.

℟. **Amen.**

Or another text from the rite of funerals may be used.

CHAPTER VII

TEXTS FOR USE
IN THE RITES FOR THE SICK

I. BIBLICAL READINGS

152. The following readings may be used in the Mass for the sick, in the visitation of the sick (the rite for one person or for several), or when praying for the sick whether they are present or absent. The selection should be made according to pastoral need, and special attention should be given to the physical and spiritual condition of the sick persons for whom the readings are used. Certain readings are indicated as more suitable for the dying.

Readings from the Old Testament

153.   1 Kings 19:1-8

A reading from the first book of Kings

Elijah was comforted and protected on his journey by the Lord

In those days Ahab told Jezebel all that Elijah had done, and how he had slain all the prophets with the sword. Then Jezebel sent a messenger to Elijah, saying, "So may the gods do to me and

more also, if I do not make your life as the life of one of them by this time tomorrow." Then he was afraid, and he arose and went for his life, and came to Beer-sheba, which belongs to Judah, and left his servant there.

But he himself went a day's journey into the wilderness, and came and sat down under a broom tree; and he asked that he might die, saying, "It is enough; now, O Lord, take away my life; for I am no better than my fathers."

And he lay down and slept under a broom tree; and behold, an angel touched him, and said to him, "Arise and eat." And he looked and behold, there was at his head a cake baked on hot stones and a jar of water. And he ate and drank, and lay down again. And the angel of the Lord came again a second time, and touched him, and said, "Arise and eat, else the journey will be too great for you." And he arose, and ate and drank, and went in the strength of that food forty days and forty nights to Horeb the mount of God.

This is the Word of the Lord.

154.   Job 3:1-3, 11-17, 20-23

A reading from the book of Job

Why should the sufferer be born to see the light?

Job opened his mouth and cursed the day of his birth. And Job said:

"Let the day perish wherein I was born,
   and the night which said,
      'A man-child is conceived.'

"Why did I not die at birth,
   come forth from the womb and expire?
Why did the knees receive me?
   Or why the breasts, that I should suck?
For then I should have lain down and been quiet;
   I should have slept; then I should have been at
      rest,
with kings and counselors of the earth
   who rebuilt ruins for themselves,
or with princes who had gold,
   who filled their houses with silver.
Or why was I not as a hidden untimely birth,
   as infants that never see the light?
There the wicked cease from troubling,
   and there the weary are at rest.

"Why is light given to him that is in misery,
   and life to the bitter in soul,
who long for death, but it comes not,
   and dig for it more than for hid treasures;
who rejoice exceedingly,
   and are glad, when they find the grave?
Why is light given to a man whose way is hid,
   whom God has hedged in?"

                    This is the Word of the Lord.

155.   Job 7:1-4, 6-11

A reading from the book of Job

Remember that my life is like the wind

In those days Job spoke, saying:
"Has not man a hard service upon earth,
   and are not his days like the days of a hireling?
Like a slave who longs for the shadow,
   and like a hireling who looks for his wages,
so I am allotted months of emptiness,
   and nights of misery are apportioned to me.
When I lie down I say, 'When shall I arise?'
   But the night is long,
   and I am full of tossing till the dawn.
My days are swifter than a weaver's shuttle,
   and come to their end without hope.
Remember that my life is a breath;
   my eye will never again see good.
The eye of him who sees me will behold me no
      more;
   while thy eyes are upon me, I shall be gone.
As the cloud fades and vanishes,
   so he who goes down to Sheol does not come
      up;
he returns no more to his house,
   nor does his place know him any more.

"Therefore I will not restrain my mouth;
   I will speak in the anguish of my spirit;
   I will complain in the bitterness of my soul."

                          This is the Word of the Lord.

156.   Job 7:12-21

A reading from the book of Job

What is man, that you make much of him?

In those days Job spoke, saying:
"Am I the sea, or a sea monster,
  that thou settest a guard over me?
When I say, 'My bed will comfort me,
  my couch will ease my complaint,'
then thou dost scare me with dreams
  and terrify me with visions,
so that I would choose strangling
  and death rather than my bones.
I loathe my life; I would not live for ever.
  Let me alone, for my days are a breath.
What is man, that thou dost make so much of him,
  and that thou dost set thy mind upon him,
dost visit him every morning,
  and test him every moment?
How long wilt thou not look away from me,
  nor let me alone till I swallow my spittle?
If I sin, what do I do to thee, thou watcher of men?
  Why hast thou made me thy mark?
  Why have I become a burden to thee?
Why dost thou not pardon my transgression
  and take away my iniquity?
For now I shall lie in the earth;
  thou wilt seek me, but I shall not be."

                          This is the Word of the Lord.

157.   (For the dying)   Job 19:23-27a

A reading from the book of Job

I know that my redeemer lives

In those days Job spoke, saying:
"Oh that my words were written!
  Oh that they were inscribed in a book!
Oh that with an iron pen and lead
  they were graven in the rock for ever!
For I know that my Redeemer lives,
  and at last he will stand upon the earth;
and after my skin has been thus destroyed,
  then from my flesh I shall see God,
whom I shall see on my side,
  and my eyes shall behold, and not another.

This is the Word of the Lord.

158.   Wisdom 9:9-11, 13-18

A reading from the book of Wisdom

Who could know your counsel unless you had
given him wisdom?

O God of my fathers and Lord of mercy,
with thee is wisdom, who knows thy works
and was present when thou didst make the world,
and who understands what is pleasing in thy sight
and what is right according to thy commandments.
Send her forth from the holy heavens,
and from the throne of thy glory send her,
that she may be with me and toil,

and that I may learn what is pleasing to thee.
For she knows and understands all things,
and she will guide me wisely in my actions
and guard me with her glory.
What man can learn the counsel of God?
Or who can discern what the Lord wills?
For the reasoning of mortals is worthless,
and our designs are likely to fail,
for a perishable body weighs down the soul,
and this earthy tent burdens the thoughtful mind.
We can hardly guess at what is on earth,
and what is at hand we find with labor;
but who has traced out what is in the heavens?
Who has learned thy counsel, unless thou hast
  given wisdom
and sent thy holy Spirit from on high?
And thus the paths of those on earth were set right,
and men were taught what pleases thee,
and were saved by wisdom.

This is the Word of the Lord.

159.   Isaiah 35:1-10

A reading from the book of the prophet Isaiah

Strengthen the feeble hands

The wilderness and the dry land shall be glad,
  the desert shall rejoice and blossom;
like the crocus it shall blossom abundantly,
  and rejoice with joy and singing.
The glory of Lebanon shall be given to it,
  the majesty of Carmel and Sharon.

They shall see the glory of the Lord,
  the majesty of our God.

Strengthen the weak hands,
  and make firm the feeble knees.
Say to those who are of a fearful heart,
  "Be strong, fear not!
Behold, your God
  will come with vengeance,
with the recompense of God.
  He will come and save you."

Then the eyes of the blind shall be opened,
  and the ears of the deaf unstopped;
then shall the lame man leap like a hart,
  and the tongue of the dumb sing for joy.

For waters shall break forth in the wilderness,
  and streams in the desert;
the burning sand shall become a pool,
  and the thirsty ground springs of water;
the haunt of jackals shall become a swamp,
  the grass shall become reeds and rushes.

And a highway shall be there,
  and it shall be called the Holy Way;
the unclean shall not pass over it,
  and fools shall not err therein.
No lion shall be there,
  nor shall any ravenous beast come up on it;
they shall not be found there,
  but the redeemed shall walk there.
And the ransomed of the Lord shall return,

and come to Zion with singing;
everlasting joy shall be upon their heads;
  they shall obtain joy and gladness,
  and sorrow and sighing shall flee away.

This is the Word of the Lord.

160.   Isaiah 52:13—53:12

A reading from the book of the prophet Isaiah

He bore our sufferings himself

Behold, my servant shall prosper,
  he shall be exalted and lifted up,
    and shall be very high.
As many were astonished at him —
  his appearance was so marred, beyond human
    semblance,
    and his form beyond that of the sons of men —
so shall he startle many nations;
  kings shall shut their mouths because of him;
for that which has not been told them they shall see,
  and that which they have not heard they shall
    understand.

Who has believed what we have heard?
  And to whom has the arm of the Lord been
    revealed?
For he grew up before him like a young plant,
  and like a root out of dry ground;
he had no form or comeliness that we should look
    at him,
  and no beauty that we should desire him.

He was despised and rejected by men;
　　a man of sorrows, and acquainted with grief;
and as one from whom men hide their faces
　　he was despised, and we esteemed him not.

Surely he has borne our griefs
　　and carried our sorrows;
yet we esteemed him stricken,
　　smitten by God, and afflicted.
But he was wounded for our transgressions,
　　he was bruised for our iniquities;
upon him was the chastisement that made us
　　　whole,
　　and with his stripes we are healed.
All we like sheep have gone astray;
　　we have turned every one to his own way;
and the Lord has laid on him
　　the iniquity of us all.

He was oppressed, and he was afflicted,
　　yet he opened not his mouth;
like a lamb that is led to the slaughter,
　　and like a sheep that before its shearers is
　　　dumb,
　　so he opened not his mouth.
By oppression and judgment he was taken away;
　　and as for his generation, who considered
that he was cut off out of the land of the living,
　　stricken for the transgression of my people?
And they made his grave with the wicked
　　and with a rich man in his death,
although he had done no violence,
　　and there was no deceit in his mouth.

Yet it was the will of the Lord to bruise him;
   he has put him to grief;
when he makes himself an offering for sin,
   he shall see his offspring, he shall prolong his
      days;
the will of the Lord shall prosper in his hand;
   he shall see the fruit of the travail of his soul
      and be satisfied;
by his knowledge shall the righteous one, my
    servant,
   make many to be accounted righteous;
   and he shall bear their iniquities.
Therefore I will divide him a portion with the great,
   and he shall divide the spoil with the strong;
because he poured out his soul to death,
   and was numbered with the transgressors;
yet he bore the sin of many,
   and made intercession for the transgressors.

This is the Word of the Lord.

161.   Isaiah 61:1-3a

A reading from the book of the prophet Isaiah

The spirit of the Lord is upon me
to comfort all who mourn

The Spirit of the Lord God is upon me,
   because the Lord has anointed me
to bring good tidings to the afflicted;
   he has sent me to bind up the brokenhearted,
to proclaim liberty to the captives,

and the opening of the prison to those who are
   bound;
to proclaim the year of the Lord's favor,
   and the day of vengeance of our God;
   to comfort all who mourn;
to grant to those who mourn in Zion—
   to give them a garland instead of ashes,
the oil of gladness instead of mourning,
   the mantle of praise instead of a faint spirit.

This is the Word of the Lord.

Readings from the New Testament

162.   Acts 3:1-10

A reading from the Acts of the Apostles

In the name of Jesus arise and walk

**Peter and John were going up to the temple at
the hour of prayer, the ninth hour. And a man lame
from birth was being carried, whom they laid daily
at that gate of the temple which is called Beautiful
to ask alms of those who entered the temple. Seeing Peter and John about to go into the temple, he
asked for alms. And Peter directed his gaze at
him, with John, and said, "Look at us." And he
fixed his attention upon them, expecting to receive
something from them. But Peter said, "I have no
silver and gold, but I give you what I have; in the
name of Jesus Christ of Nazareth, walk." And he**

took him by the right hand and raised him up; and immediately his feet and ankles were made strong. And leaping up he stood and walked and entered the temple with them, walking and leaping and praising God. And all the people saw him walking and praising God, and recognized him as the one who sat for alms at the Beautiful Gate of the temple; and they were filled with wonder and amazement at what had happened to him.

This is the Word of the Lord.

163. Acts 3:11-16

A reading from the Acts of the Apostles

Faith in God has given this man perfect health

While the lame man who had been cured clung to Peter and John, all the people ran together to them in the portico called Solomon's, astounded. And when Peter saw it he addressed the people, "Men of Israel, why do you wonder at this, or why do you stare at us, as though by our own power or piety we had made him walk? The God of Abraham and of Isaac and of Jacob, the God of our fathers, glorified his servant Jesus, whom you delivered up and denied in the presence of Pilate, when he had decided to release him. But you denied the Holy and Righteous One, and asked for a murderer to be granted to you, and killed the Author of life, whom God raised from the dead. To this we are witnesses. And his name, by faith in his name, has made this man strong whom you see

and know; and the faith which is through Jesus
has given the man this perfect health in the presence of you all.

This is the Word of the Lord.

164.   Acts 4:8-12

A reading from the Acts of the Apostles

There is no other name by which we are saved

**Peter, filled with the Holy Spirit, said, "Rulers of
the people and elders, if we are being examined
today concerning a good deed done to a cripple,
by what means this man has been healed, be it
known to you all, and to all the people of Israel,
that by the name of Jesus Christ of Nazareth,
whom you crucified, whom God raised from the
dead, by him this man is standing before you well.
This is the stone which was rejected by you build-
ers, but which has become the head of the corner.
And there is salvation in no one else, for there is
no other name under heaven given among men by
which we must be saved."**

This is the Word of the Lord.

165.   Acts 13:32-39

A reading from the Acts of the Apostles

The one whom God raised from the dead
will never see corruption of the flesh

**In those days Paul said, "We bring you the good
news that what God promised to the fathers, this**

he has fulfilled to us their children by raising Jesus; as also it is written in the second psalm,

'Thou art my Son,
    today I have begotten thee.'

"And as for the fact that he raised him from the dead, no more to return to corruption, he spoke in this way,

'I will give you the holy and sure blessings of
    David.'

"Therefore he says also in another psalm,

'Thou wilt not let thy Holy One see corruption.'

"For David, after he had served the counsel of God in his own generation, fell asleep, and was laid with his fathers, and saw corruption; but he whom God raised up saw no corruption. Let it be known to you therefore, brethren, that through this man forgiveness of sins is proclaimed to you, and by him every one that believes is freed from everything from which you could not be freed by the law of Moses."

This is the Word of the Lord.

166.   Romans 8:14-17

A reading from the letter of Paul to the Romans

If we suffer with him, we will be glorified with him

Brethren, all who are led by the Spirit of God are sons of God. For you did not receive the spirit of slavery to fall back into fear, but you have received the spirit of sonship. When we cry, "Abba! Father!"

it is the Spirit himself bearing witness with our spirit that we are children of God, and if children, then heirs, heirs of God and fellow heirs with Christ, provided we suffer with him in order that we may also be glorified with him.

                    This is the Word of the Lord.

167.   Romans 8:18-27

A reading from the letter of Paul to the Romans

We groan while we wait for the redemption of our bodies

Brethren, I consider that the sufferings of this present time are not worth comparing with the glory that is to be revealed to us. For the creation waits with eager longing for the revealing of the sons of God; for the creation was subjected to futility, not of its own will but by the will of him who subjected it in hope; because the creation itself will be set free from its bondage to decay and obtain the glorious liberty of the children of God. We know that the whole creation has been groaning in travail together until now; and not only the creation, but we ourselves, who have the first fruits of the Spirit, groan inwardly as we wait for adoption as sons, the redemption of our bodies. For in this hope we were saved. Now hope that is seen is not hope. For who hopes for what he sees? But if we hope for what we do not see, we wait for it with patience.

Likewise the Spirit helps us in our weakness;

for we do not know how to pray as we ought, but the Spirit himself intercedes for us with sighs too deep for words. And he who searches the hearts of men knows what is the mind of the Spirit, because the Spirit intercedes for the saints according to the will of God.

This is the Word of the Lord.

168.   Romans 8:31b-35, 37-39

A reading from the letter of Paul to the Romans

Who can come between us and the love of Christ?

If God is for us, who is against us? He who did not spare his own Son but gave him up for us all, will he not also give us all things with him? Who shall bring any charge against God's elect? It is God who justifies; who is to condemn? Is it Christ Jesus, who died, yes, who was raised from the dead, who is at the right hand of God, who indeed intercedes for us? Who shall separate us from the love of Christ? Shall tribulation, or distress, or persecution, or famine, or nakedness, or peril, or sword?

No, in all these things we are more than conquerors through him who loved us. For I am sure that neither death, nor life, nor angels, nor principalities, nor things present, nor things to come, nor powers, nor height nor depth nor anything else in all creation will be able to separate us from the love of God in Christ Jesus our Lord.

This is the Word of the Lord.

169.   1 Corinthians 1:18-25

A reading from the first letter of Paul to the Corinthians

God's weakness is stronger than man's strength

The word of the cross is folly to those who are perishing, but to us who are being saved it is the power of God. For it is written,

"I will destroy the wisdom of the wise,
and the cleverness of the clever I will thwart."

Where is the wise man? Where is the scribe? Where is the debater of this age? Has not God made foolish the wisdom of the world? For since, in the wisdom of God, the world did not know God through wisdom, it pleased God through the folly of what we preach to save those who believe. For Jews demand signs and Greeks seek wisdom, but we preach Christ crucified, a stumbling block to Jews and folly to Gentiles, but to those who are called, both Jews and Greeks, Christ the power of God and the wisdom of God. For the foolishness of God is wiser than men, and the weakness of God is stronger than men.

This is the Word of the Lord.

170.   1 Corinthians 12:12-22, 24b-27

A reading from the first letter of Paul to the Corinthians

If one member suffers, all the members suffer with him

Brethren, just as the body is one and has many members, and all the members of the body, though many, are one body, so it is with Christ. For by one Spirit we were all baptized into one body — Jews or Greeks, slaves or free — and all were made to drink of one Spirit.

For the body does not consist of one member but of many. If the foot should say, "Because I am not a hand, I do not belong to the body," that would not make it any less a part of the body. And if the ear should say, "Because I am not an eye, I do not belong to the body," that would not make it any less a part of the body. If the whole body were an eye, where would be the hearing? If the whole body were an ear, where would be the sense of smell?

But as it is, God arranged the organs in the body, each one of them, as he chose. If all were a single organ, where would the body be? As it is, there are many parts, yet one body. The eye cannot say to the hand, "I have no need of you," nor again the head to the feet, "I have no need of you."

On the contrary, the parts of the body which seem to be weaker are indispensable. But God has so adjusted the body, giving the greater honor to the inferior part, that there may be no discord in the body, but that the members may have the same care for one another. If one member suffers, all suffer together; if one member is honored, all rejoice together.

Now you are the body of Christ and individually members of it.

This is the Word of the Lord.

171.   (For the dying)   1 Corinthians 15:12-20

A reading from the first letter of Paul to the Corinthians

If there is no resurrection from the dead,
Christ himself has not risen

If Christ is preached as raised from the dead how can some of you say that there is no resurrection of the dead? But if there is no resurrection of the dead, then Christ has not been raised; if Christ has not been raised, then our preaching is in vain and your faith is in vain. We are even found to be misrepresenting God, because we testified of God that he raised Christ, whom he did not raise if it is true that the dead are not raised. For if the dead are not raised, then Christ has not been raised. If Christ has not been raised, your faith is futile and you are still in your sins. Then those also who have fallen asleep in Christ have perished. If for this life only we have hoped in Christ, we are of all men most to be pitied.

But in fact Christ has been raised from the dead, the first fruits of those who have fallen asleep.

This is the Word of the Lord.

172.   2 Corinthians 4:16-18

A reading from the second letter of Paul to the Corinthians

*Though our body is being destroyed,
each day it is also being renewed*

Brethren, we do not lose heart. Though our outer nature is wasting away, our inner nature is being renewed every day. For this slight momentary affliction is preparing for us an eternal weight of glory beyond all comparison, because we look not to the things that are seen but to the things that are unseen; for the things that are seen are transient, but the things that are unseen are eternal.

This is the Word of the Lord.

173.   (For the dying)   2 Corinthians 5:1, 6-10

A reading from the second letter of Paul to the Corinthians

We have an everlasting home in heaven

We know that if the earthly tent we live in is destroyed, we have a building from God, a house not made with hands, eternal in the heavens.

So we are always of good courage; we know that while we are at home in the body we are away from the Lord, for we walk by faith, not by sight.

We are of good courage, and we would rather be away from the body and at home with the Lord. So whether we are at home or away, we make it our aim to please him. For we must all appear before the judgment seat of Christ, so that each one may receive good or evil, according to what he has done in the body.

This is the Word of the Lord.

174.   Galatians 4:12-19

A reading from the letter of Paul to the Galatians

My bodily sickness enabled me to bring the gospel to you

I beseech you, become as I am, for I also have become as you are. You did me no wrong; you know it was because of a bodily ailment that I preached the gospel to you at first; and though my condition was a trial to you, you did not scorn or despise me, but received me as an angel of God, as Christ Jesus.

What has become of the satisfaction you felt? For I bear you witness that, if possible, you would have plucked out your eyes and given them to me. Have I then become your enemy by telling you the truth? They make much of you, but for no good purpose; they want to shut you out, that you may make much of them. For a good purpose it is always good to be made much of, and not only when

I am present with you. My little children, with whom I am again in travail until Christ be formed in you!

This is the Word of the Lord.

175.   Philippians 2:25-30

A reading from the letter of Paul to the Philippians

He was sick but God took pity on him

I have thought it necessary to send to you Epaphroditus my brother and fellow worker and fellow soldier, and your messenger and minister to my need, for he has been longing for you all, and has been distressed because you heard that he was ill. Indeed he was ill, near to death. But God had mercy on him, and not only on him but on me also, lest I should have sorrow upon sorrow.

I am the more eager to send him, therefore, that you may rejoice at seeing him again, and that I may be less anxious. So receive him in the Lord with all joy; and honor such men, for he nearly died for the work of Christ, risking his life to complete your service to me.

This is the Word of the Lord.

176.   Colossians 1:22-29

A reading from the letter of Paul to the Colossians

In my flesh I fill up what is lacking in the sufferings of Christ for the sake of his body

Christ has now reconciled you in his body of flesh by his death, in order to present you holy and blameless and irreproachable before him, provided that you continue in the faith, stable and steadfast, not shifting from the hope of the gospel which you heard, which has been preached to every creature under heaven, and of which I, Paul, became a minister.

Now I rejoice in my sufferings for your sake, and in my flesh I complete what is lacking in Christ's afflictions for the sake of his body, that is, the church, of which I became a minister according to the divine office which was given to me for you, to make the word of God fully known, the mystery hidden for ages and generations but now made manifest to his saints. To them God chose to make known how great among the Gentiles are the riches of the glory of this mystery, which is Christ in you, the hope of glory. Him we proclaim, warning every man and teaching every man in all wisdom, that we may present every man mature in Christ. For this I toil, striving with all the energy which he mightily inspires within me.

This is the Word of the Lord.

177.   Hebrews 4:14-16; 5:7-9

A reading from the letter to the Hebrews

We do not have a high priest
who does not understand our sickness

Since we have a great high priest who has passed through the heavens, Jesus, the Son of God, let us hold fast our confession. For we have not a high priest who is unable to sympathize with our weaknesses, but one who in every respect has been tempted as we are, yet without sinning. Let us then with confidence draw near to the throne of grace, that we may receive mercy and find grace to help in time of need.

In the days of his flesh, Jesus offered up prayers and supplications, with loud cries and tears, to him who was able to save him from death, and he was heard for his godly fear. Although he was a Son, he learned obedience through what he suffered; and being made perfect he became the source of eternal salvation to all who obey him.

This is the Word of the Lord.

178.   James 5:13-16

A reading from the letter of James

This prayer, made in faith, will save the sick man

Is any one among you suffering? Let him pray. Is any cheerful? Let him sing praise. Is any among you sick? Let him call for the elders of the church, and let them pray over him, anointing him with oil in the name of the Lord; and the prayer of faith will save the sick man, and the Lord will raise him up; and if he has committed sins, he will be forgiven. Therefore confess your sins to one another, and pray for one another, that you may be healed. The prayer of a righteous man has great power in its effects.

This is the Word of the Lord.

179.   1 Peter 1:3-9

A reading from the first letter of Peter

You will rejoice even though for a short time you must suffer

Blessed be the God and Father of our Lord Jesus Christ! By his great mercy we have been born anew to a living hope through the resurrection of Jesus Christ from the dead, and to an inheritance which is imperishable, undefiled, and unfading, kept in heaven for you, who by God's power are guarded through faith for a salvation ready to be revealed in the last time. In this you rejoice, though now for a little while you may have to suffer various trials, so that the genuineness of your faith, more precious than gold which though perishable is tested by fire, may redound to praise and glory and honor at the revelation of Jesus Christ. Without having seen him you love him; though you do not now see him you believe in him and rejoice with unutterable and exalted joy. As the outcome of your faith you obtain the salvation of your souls.

This is the Word of the Lord.

180.   1 John 3:1-2

A reading from the first letter of John

What we shall be has not yet been disclosed

**See what love the Father has given us, that we
should be called children of God; and so we are.
The reason why the world does not know us is
that it did not know him. Beloved, we are God's
children now; it does not yet appear what we shall
be, but we know that when he appears we shall be
like him, for we shall see him as he is.**

This is the Word of the Lord.

181.   Revelation 21:1-7

A reading from the book of Revelation

There will be no more death or mourning, crying or pain

**I, John, saw a new heaven and a new earth; for
the first heaven and the first earth had passed
away, and the sea was no more. And I saw the holy
city, new Jerusalem, coming down out of heaven
from God, prepared as a bride adorned for her
husband; and I heard a great voice from the throne
saying, "Behold, the dwelling of God is with men.
He will dwell with them, and they shall be his people, and God himself will be with them; he will
wipe away every tear from their eyes, and death
shall be no more, neither shall there be mourning
nor crying nor pain any more, for the former things
have passed away."**

And he who sat upon the throne said, "Behold, I make all things new." Also he said, "Write this, for these words are trustworthy and true." And he said to me, "It is done! I am the Alpha and the Omega, the beginning and the end. To the thirsty I will give water without price from the fountain of the water of life. He who conquers shall have this heritage, and I will be his God and he shall be my son."   **This is the Word of the Lord.**

182.   (For the dying)   Revelation 22:17, 20-21

A reading from the book of Revelation

Come, Lord Jesus

The Spirit and the Bride say, "Come." And let him who hears say, "Come." And let him who is thirsty come, let him who desires take the water of life without price.

He who testifies to these things says, "Surely I am coming soon." Amen. Come, Lord Jesus!

The grace of the Lord Jesus be with all the saints. Amen.

                    This is the Word of the Lord.

Responsorial Psalms

183.   Isaiah 38:10, 11, 12abcd, and 16

℟. **(17b) You saved my life, O Lord; I shall not die.**

I said, In the noontide of my days
    I must depart;

I am consigned to the gates of Sheol
    for the rest of my years.

℟. You saved my life, O Lord; I shall not die.

I said, I shall not see the Lord
    in the land of the living;
I shall look upon man no more
    among the inhabitants of the world.

℟. You saved my life, O Lord; I shall not die.

My dwelling is plucked up and removed from me
    like a shepherd's tent;
like a weaver I have rolled up my life;
    he cuts me off from the loom.

℟. You saved my life, O Lord; I shall not die.

O Lord, by these things men live,
    and in all these is the life of my spirit.
    Oh, restore me to health and make me live!

℟. You saved my life, O Lord; I shall not die.

184.   Psalm 6:1-3a, 3b-5, 8-9

℟. (2a) Have mercy on me, Lord; my strength is
    gone.

O Lord, rebuke me not in thy anger,
    nor chasten me in thy wrath.
Be gracious to me, O Lord, for I am languishing;
    O Lord, heal me, for my bones are troubled.
My soul also is sorely troubled.

℟. Have mercy on me, Lord; my strength is gone.

But thou, O Lord — how long?
Turn, O Lord, save my life;
   deliver me for the sake of thy steadfast love.
For in death there is no remembrance of thee;
   in Sheol who can give thee praise?

℟. Have mercy on me, Lord; my strength is gone.

Depart from me, all you workers of evil;
   for the Lord has heard the sound of my
     weeping.
The Lord has heard my supplication;
   the Lord accepts my prayer.

℟. Have mercy on me, Lord; my strength is gone.

185. Psalm 25:4-5ab, 6-7bc, 8-9, 10 and 14, 15-16

℟. (1b) To you, O Lord, I lift up my soul.

Make me to know thy ways, O Lord;
   teach me thy paths.
Lead me in thy truth, and teach me,
   for thou art the God of my salvation.

℟. To you, O Lord, I lift up my soul.

Be mindful of thy mercy, O Lord, and of thy
    steadfast love,
   for they have been from of old.
According to thy steadfast love remember me,
   for thy goodness' sake, O Lord!

℟. To you, O Lord, I lift up my soul.

Good and upright is the Lord;
  therefore he instructs sinners in the way.
He leads the humble in what is right,
  and teaches the humble his way.

℟. To you, O Lord, I lift up my soul.

All the paths of the Lord are steadfast love and
  faithfulness,
    for those who keep his covenant and his
    testimonies.
The friendship of the Lord is for those who fear
  him,
    and he makes known to them his covenant.

℟. To you, O Lord, I lift up my soul.

My eyes are ever toward the Lord,
  for he will pluck my feet out of the net.
Turn thou to me, and be gracious to me;
  for I am lonely and afflicted.

℟. To you, O Lord, I lift up my soul.

186.   Psalm 27:1, 4, 5, 7-8b-9ab, 9cd-10

℟. (14) Put your hope in the Lord; take courage
  and be strong.

The Lord is my light and my salvation;
  whom shall I fear?
The Lord is the stronghold of my life;
  of whom shall I be afraid?

℟. Put your hope in the Lord; take courage and be
  strong.

One thing have I asked of the Lord,
   that will I seek after;
that I may dwell in the house of the Lord
   all the days of my life,
to behold the beauty of the Lord,
   and to inquire in his temple.

℟. Put your hope in the Lord; take courage and be
     strong.

For he will hide me in his shelter
   in the day of trouble;
he will conceal me under the cover of his tent,
   he will set me high upon a rock.

℟. Put your hope in the Lord; take courage and be
     strong.

Hear, O Lord, when I cry aloud,
   be gracious to me and answer me!
   My heart says to thee,
"Thy face, Lord, do I seek."
   Hide not thy face from me.
Turn not thy servant away in anger,
   thou who hast been my help.

℟. Put your hope in the Lord; take courage and be
     strong.

Cast me not off, forsake me not,
   O God of my salvation!
For my father and my mother have forsaken me,
   but the Lord will take me up.

℟. Put your hope in the Lord; take courage and be
     strong.

187. Psalm 34:1-2, 3-4, 5-6, 9-10, 11-12, 16 and 18

℟. **(18a) The Lord is near to broken hearts.**
    or **(8a) Taste and see the goodness of the
        Lord.**

I will bless the Lord at all times;
    his praise shall continually be in my mouth.
My soul makes its boast in the Lord;
    let the afflicted hear and be glad.

℟. **The Lord is near to broken hearts.**
    or **Taste and see the goodness of the Lord.**

O magnify the Lord with me,
    and let us exalt his name together!
I sought the Lord and he answered me,
    and delivered me from all my fears.

℟. **The Lord is near to broken hearts.**
    or **Taste and see the goodness of the Lord.**

Look to him, and be radiant;
    so your faces shall never be ashamed.
This poor man cried, and the Lord heard him,
    and saved him out of all his troubles.

℟. **The Lord is near to broken hearts.**
    or **Taste and see the goodness of the Lord.**

O fear the Lord, you his saints,
    for those who fear him have no want!
The young lions suffer want and hunger;
    but those who seek the Lord lack no good
        thing.

℟. **The Lord is near to broken hearts.**
     or **Taste and see the goodness of the Lord.**

Come, O sons, listen to me,
     I will teach you the fear of the Lord.
What man is there who desires life,
     and covets many days, that he may enjoy
       good?

℟. **The Lord is near to broken hearts.**
     or **Taste and see the goodness of the Lord.**

The face of the Lord is against evildoers,
     to cut off the remembrance of them from the
       earth.
The Lord is near to the broken-hearted,
     and saves the crushed in spirit.

℟. **The Lord is near to broken hearts.**
     or **Taste and see the goodness of the Lord.**

188.   Psalm 42:2, 4; Psalm 42:3, 4

℟. **(1) Like a deer that longs for running streams,**
     my soul longs for you, my God.

My soul thirsts for God,
     for the living God.
When shall I come and behold
     the face of God?

℟. **Like a deer that longs for running streams,**
     my soul longs for you, my God.

These things I remember,
     as I pour out my soul:

how I went with the throng,
   and led them in procession to the house of
      God,
with glad shouts and songs of thanksgiving,
   a multitude keeping festival.

℟. Like a deer that longs for running streams,
   my soul longs for you, my God.

Oh send out thy light and thy truth;
   let them lead me,
let them bring me to thy holy hill
   and to thy dwelling!

℟. Like a deer that longs for running streams,
   my soul longs for you, my God.

Then I will go to the altar of God,
   to God my exceeding joy;
and I will praise thee with the lyre,
   O God, my God.

℟. Like a deer that longs for running streams,
   my soul longs for you, my God.

189.   Psalm 63:1-2, 3-5, 6-8

℟. (1b) My soul is thirsting for you, O Lord my God.

O God, thou art my God, I seek thee,
   my soul thirsts for thee;
my flesh faints for thee,
   as in a dry and weary land where no water is.
So I have looked upon thee in the sanctuary,
   beholding thy power and glory.

℟. My soul is thirsting for you, O Lord my God.

Because thy steadfast love is better than life,
    my lips will praise thee.
So I will bless thee as long as I live;
    I will lift up my hands and call on thy name.
My soul is feasted as with marrow and fat,
    and my mouth praises thee with joyful lips.

℟. My soul is thirsting for you, O Lord my God.

When I think of thee upon my bed,
    and meditate on thee in the watches of the
        night;
for thou hast been my help,
    and in the shadow of thy wings I sing for joy.
My soul clings to thee;
    thy right hand upholds me.

℟. My soul is thirsting for you, O Lord my God.

190.   Psalm 71:1-2, 5-6ab, 8-9, 14-15ab

℟. (12b) My God, come quickly to help me.
        or (23) My lips, my very soul will shout for joy;
        you have redeemed me!

In thee, O Lord, do I take refuge;
    let me never be put to shame!
In thy righteousness deliver me and rescue me;
    incline thy ear to me, and save me!

℟. My God, come quickly to help me.
        or My lips, my very soul will shout for joy;
        you have redeemed me!

For thou, O Lord, art my hope,
  my trust, O Lord, from my youth.
Upon thee I have leaned from my birth;
  thou art he who took me from my mother's
    womb.
My praise is continually of thee.

℟. My God, come quickly to help me.
    or My lips, my very soul will shout for joy;
    you have redeemed me!

My mouth is filled with thy praise,
  and with thy glory all the day.
Do not cast me off in the time of old age;
  forsake me not when my strength is spent.

℟. My God, come quickly to help me.
    or My lips, my very soul will shout for joy;
    you have redeemed me!

But I will hope continually,
  and will praise thee yet more and more.
My mouth will tell of thy righteous acts,
  of thy deeds of salvation all the day.

℟. My God, come quickly to help me.
    or My lips, my very soul will shout for joy;
    you have redeemed me!

191.   Psalm 86:1-2, 3-4, 5-6, 11, 12-13, 15-16ab

℟. (1a) Listen, Lord, and answer me.
    or (15a and 16a) God, you are merciful and
    kind; turn to me and have mercy.

Incline thy ear, O Lord, and answer me,
   for I am poor and needy.
Preserve my life, for I am godly;
   save thy servant who trusts in thee.

℟. Listen, Lord, and answer me.
   or God, you are merciful and kind;
      turn to me and have mercy.

Be gracious to me, O Lord,
   for to thee do I cry all the day.
Gladden the soul of thy servant,
   for to thee, O Lord, do I lift up my soul.

℟. Listen, Lord, and answer me.
   or God, you are merciful and kind;
      turn to me and have mercy.

For thou, O Lord, art good and forgiving,
   abounding in steadfast love to all who call
      on thee.
Give ear, O Lord, to my prayer;
   hearken to my cry of supplication.

℟. Listen, Lord, and answer me.
   or God, you are merciful and kind;
      turn to me and have mercy.

Teach me thy way, O Lord,
   that I may walk in thy truth;
   unite my heart to fear thy name.

℟. Listen, Lord, and answer me.
   or God, you are merciful and kind;
      turn to me and have mercy.

I give thanks to thee, O Lord my God,
  with my whole heart,
  and I will glorify thy name for ever.
For great is thy steadfast love toward me;
  thou hast delivered my soul from the depths
    of Sheol.

℟. Listen, Lord, and answer me.
      or God, you are merciful and kind;
        turn to me and have mercy.

But thou, O Lord, art a God merciful and
    gracious,
  slow to anger and abounding in steadfast
    love and faithfulness.
Turn to me and take pity on me;
  give thy strength to thy servant.

℟. Listen, Lord, and answer me.
      or God, you are merciful and kind;
        turn to me and have mercy.

192.
Psalm 90:2, 3-4, 5-6, 9-10ab, 10cd and 12, 14 and 16

℟. (1) In every age, O Lord, you have been our
    refuge.

Before the mountains were brought forth,
  or ever thou hadst formed the earth and the
    world,
  from everlasting to everlasting thou art God.

℟. In every age, O Lord, you have been our refuge.

Thou turnest man back to the dust,
  and sayest, "Turn back, O children of men!"
For a thousand years in thy sight
  are but as yesterday when it is past,
  or as a watch in the night.

℞. In every age, O Lord, you have been our refuge.

Thou dost sweep men away; they are like a
    dream,
  like grass which is renewed in the morning:
in the morning it flourishes and is renewed;
  in the evening it fades and withers.

℞. In every age, O Lord, you have been our refuge.

For all our days pass away under thy wrath,
  our years come to an end like a sigh.
The years of our life are threescore and ten,
  or even by reason of strength fourscore.

℞. In every age, O Lord, you have been our refuge.

Yet their span is but toil and trouble;
  they are soon gone, and we fly away.
So teach us to number our days
  that we may get a heart of wisdom.

℞. In every age, O Lord, you have been our refuge.

Satisfy us in the morning with thy steadfast love,
  that we may rejoice and be glad all our days.
Let thy work be manifest to thy servants,
  and thy glorious power to their children.

℞. In every age, O Lord, you have been our refuge.

193. Psalm 102:1-2, 23-24, 25-27, 18-20

℟. (1) O Lord, hear my prayer, and let my cry come to you.

Hear my prayer, O Lord;
  let my cry come to thee!
Do not hide thy face from me
  in the day of my distress!
Incline thy ear to me;
  answer me speedily in the day when I call!

℟. O Lord, hear my prayer, and let my cry come to you.

He has broken my strength in mid-course;
  he has shortened my days.
"O my God," I say, "take me not hence
  in the midst of my days,
thou whose years endure
  throughout all generations!"

℟. O Lord, hear my prayer, and let my cry come to you.

Of old thou didst lay the foundation of the earth,
  and the heavens are the work of thy hands.
They will perish, but thou dost endure;
  they will all wear out like a garment.
Thou changest them like raiment, and they
  pass away;
  but thou art the same, and thy years have no
  end.

℟. O Lord, hear my prayer, and let my cry come to you.

Let this be recorded for a generation to come,
     so that a people yet unborn may praise the
          Lord:
that he looked down from his holy height,
     from heaven the Lord looked at the earth,
to hear the groans of the prisoners,
     to set free those who were doomed to die.

℞. O Lord, hear my prayer, and let my cry come to
     you.

194.
     Psalm 103:1-2, 3-4, 11-12, 13-14, 15-16, 17-18

℞. (1a) Oh, bless the Lord, my soul.
     or (8) The Lord is kind and merciful;
          slow to anger, and rich in compassion.

Bless the Lord, O my soul;
     and all that is within me, bless his holy name!
Bless the Lord, O my soul,
     and forget not all his benefits.

℞. Oh, bless the Lord, my soul.
     or The Lord is kind and merciful;
          slow to anger, and rich in compassion.

Who forgives all your iniquity,
     who heals all your diseases,
who redeems your life from the Pit,
     who crowns you with steadfast love and
          mercy.

℞. Oh, bless the Lord, my soul.
     or The Lord is kind and merciful;
          slow to anger, and rich in compassion.

For as the heavens are high above the earth,
   so great is his steadfast love toward those
      who fear him;
as far as the east is from the west,
   so far does he remove our transgressions
      from us.

℟. Oh, bless the Lord, my soul.
   or The Lord is kind and merciful;
      slow to anger, and rich in compassion.

As a father pities his children,
   so the Lord pities those who fear him.
For he knows our frame;
   he remembers that we are dust.

℟. Oh, bless the Lord, my soul.
   or The Lord is kind and merciful;
      slow to anger, and rich in compassion.

As for man, his days are like grass;
   he flourishes like a flower of the field;
for the wind passes over it, and it is gone,
   and its place knows it no more.

℟. Oh, bless the Lord, my soul.
   or The Lord is kind and merciful;
      slow to anger, and rich in compassion.

But the steadfast love of the Lord is from ever-
      lasting to everlasting
   upon those who fear him,
   and his righteousness to children's children,
to those who keep his covenant
   and remember to do his commandments.

℞. **Oh, bless the Lord, my soul.**
> or **The Lord is kind and merciful;
> slow to anger, and rich in compassion.**

195.   Psalm 123:1-2a, 2bcd

℞. **(2) Our eyes are fixed on the Lord, pleading for his mercy.**

**To thee I lift up my eyes,
> O thou who art enthroned in the heavens!
Behold, as the eyes of servants
> look to the hand of their master,**

℞. **Our eyes are fixed on the Lord, pleading for his mercy.**

**As the eyes of a maid
> to the hand of her mistress,
so our eyes look to the Lord our God,
> till he have mercy upon us.**

℞. **Our eyes are fixed on the Lord, pleading for his mercy.**

196.   Psalm 143:1-2, 5-6, 10

℞. **(1a) O Lord, hear my prayer.**
> or **(11a) For the sake of your name, O Lord, save my life.**

Hear my prayer, O Lord; give ear to my supplications!

In thy faithfulness answer me, in thy righteousness!
Enter not into judgment with thy servant;
   for no man living is righteous before thee.

℟. O Lord, hear my prayer.
   or For the sake of your name, O Lord, save
      my life.

I remember the days of old,
   I meditate on all that thou hast done;
   I muse on what thy hands have wrought.
I stretch out my hands to thee;
   my soul thirsts for thee like a parched land.

℟. O Lord, hear my prayer.
   or For the sake of your name, O Lord, save
      my life.

Teach me to do thy will,
   for thou art my God!
Let thy good spirit lead me
   on a level path!

℟. O Lord, hear my prayer.
   or For the sake of your name, O Lord, save
      my life.

Alleluia Verse and Verse before the Gospel

Outside of Lent, the cantor sings Alleluia; it is
then repeated by the people. The cantor then sings
one of the verses given below, and the people re-
peat Alleluia.

During Lent, the same pattern is followed, except that one of the following invocations replaces the Alleluia:

(a) **Praise to you, Lord Jesus Christ, king of endless glory!**

(b) **Praise and honor to you, Lord Jesus Christ!**

(c) **Glory and praise to you, Lord Jesus Christ!**

(d) **Glory to you, Word of God, Lord Jesus Christ!**

197.   Psalm 32:22

**Lord, let your mercy be on us,
as we place our trust in you.**

198.   Matthew 5:4

**Happy are they who mourn;
they shall be comforted.**

199.   Matthew 8:17

**He took our sickness away
and carried our diseases for us.**

200.   Matthew 11:28

**Come to me, all you that labor and are burdened,
and I will give you rest, says the Lord.**

201.   2 Corinthians 1:3b-4a

**Blessed be the Father of mercies and the God of all comfort,
who consoles us in all our afflictions.**

202.   Ephesians 1:3

Blessed be God, the Father of our Lord Jesus Christ,

for he has blessed us with every spiritual gift in
Christ.

203. James 1:12

Happy the man who stands firm when trials come;
he has proved himself, and will win the crown of
life.

Gospels

204. Matthew 5:1-12a

A reading from the holy gospel according
to Matthew

Rejoice and be glad, for your reward is great in heaven

Seeing the crowds, Jesus went up on the mountain, and when he sat down his disciples came to
him. And he opened his mouth and taught them,
saying:

"Blessed are the poor in spirit, for theirs is the
kingdom of heaven.

"Blessed are those who mourn, for they shall be
comforted.

"Blessed are the meek, for they shall inherit the
earth.

"Blessed are those who hunger and thirst for
righteousness, for they shall be satisfied.

"Blessed are the merciful, for they shall obtain
mercy.

"Blessed are the pure in heart, for they shall see God.

"Blessed are the peacemakers, for they shall be called sons of God.

"Blessed are those who are persecuted for righteousness' sake, for theirs is the kingdom of heaven.

"Blessed are you when men revile you and persecute you and utter all kinds of evil against you falsely on my account. Rejoice and be glad, for your reward is great in heaven."

This is the gospel of the Lord.

205.   Matthew 8:1-4

A reading from the holy gospel according to Matthew

If you wish to do so, you can cure me

When Jesus came down from the mountain, great crowds followed him; and behold, a leper came to him and knelt before him, saying, "Lord, if you will, you can make me clean."

And he stretched out his hand and touched him, saying, "I will; be clean." And immediately his leprosy was cleansed. And Jesus said to him, "See that you say nothing to any one; but go, show yourself to the priest, and offer the gift that Moses commanded, for a proof to the people."

This is the gospel of the Lord.

206a.   (long form)   Matthew 8:5-17

A reading from the holy gospel according to Matthew

He bore our infirmities

As Jesus entered Capernaum, a centurion came forward to him, beseeching him and saying, "Lord, my servant is lying paralyzed at home, in terrible distress."

And he said to him, "I will come and heal him."

But the centurion answered him, "Lord, I am not worthy to have you come under my roof; but only say the word, and my servant will be healed. For I am a man under authority, with soldiers under me; and I say to one, 'Go,' and he goes, and to another, 'Come,' and he comes, and to my slave, 'Do this,' and he does it."

When Jesus heard him, he marveled, and said to those who followed him, "Truly, I say to you, not even in Israel have I found such faith. I tell you, many will come from east and west and sit at table with Abraham, Isaac, and Jacob in the kingdom of heaven, while the sons of the kingdom will be thrown into the outer darkness; there men will weep and gnash their teeth."

And to the centurion Jesus said, "Go; be it done for you as you have believed." And the servant was healed at that very moment.

And when Jesus entered Peter's house, he saw his mother-in-law lying sick with a fever; he touched her hand, and the fever left her, and she rose and served him. That evening they brought to him many who were possessed with demons; and he cast out the spirits with a word, and healed all who were sick. This was to fulfil what was spoken by the prophet Isaiah, "He took our infirmities and bore our diseases."

> This is the gospel of the Lord.

206b.   (short form)   Matthew 8:5-13

A reading from the holy gospel according to Matthew

He bore our infirmities

As Jesus entered Capernaum, a centurion came forward to him, beseeching him and saying, "Lord, my servant is lying paralyzed at home, in terrible distress."

And he said to him, "I will come and heal him."

But the centurion answered him, "Lord, I am not worthy to have you come under my roof; but only say the word, and my servant will be healed. For I am a man under authority, with soldiers under me; and I say to one, 'Go,' and he goes, and to another, 'Come,' and he comes, and to my slave, 'Do this,' and he does it."

When Jesus heard him, he marveled, and said to those who followed him, "Truly, I say to you, not even in Israel have I found such faith. I tell you, many will come from east and west and sit at table with Abraham, Isaac, and Jacob in the kingdom of heaven, while the sons of the kingdom will be thrown into the outer darkness; there men will weep and gnash their teeth."

And to the centurion Jesus said, "Go; be it done for you as you have believed." And the servant was healed at that very moment.

This is the gospel of the Lord.

206c.   (short form)   Matthew 8:14-17

A reading from the holy gospel according to Matthew

He bore our infirmities

When Jesus entered Peter's house, he saw his mother-in-law lying sick with a fever; he touched her hand, and the fever left her, and she rose and served him. That evening they brought to him many who were possessed with demons; and he cast out the spirits with a word, and healed all who were sick. This was to fulfil what was spoken by the prophet Isaiah, "He took our infirmities and bore our diseases."

This is the gospel of the Lord.

207.   Matthew 11:25-30

A reading from the holy gospel according to Matthew

Come to me, all you who labor

At that time Jesus declared, "I thank thee, Father, Lord of heaven and earth, that thou hast hidden these things from the wise and understanding and revealed them to babes; yea, Father, for such was thy gracious will. All things have been delivered to me by my Father; and no one knows the Son except the Father, and no one knows the Father except the Son and any one to whom the Son chooses to reveal him. Come to me, all who labor and are heavy laden, and I will give you rest. Take my yoke upon you, and learn from me; for I am gentle and lowly in heart, and you will find rest for your souls. For my yoke is easy, and my burden is light."

This is the gospel of the Lord.

208.   Matthew 15:29-31

A reading from the holy gospel according to Matthew

Jesus heals large crowds

At that time Jesus passed along the Sea of Galilee. And he went up into the hills, and sat down there. And great crowds came to him, bringing with them the lame, the maimed, the blind, the dumb, and many others, and they put them at his feet, and he healed them, so that the throng wondered, when they saw the dumb speaking, the maimed whole, the lame walking, and the blind seeing; and they glorified the God of Israel.

This is the gospel of the Lord.

209.   Matthew 25:31-40

A reading from the holy gospel according to Matthew

As often as you did it to the least of my brothers you did it to me

Jesus said to his disciples, "When the Son of man comes in his glory, and all the angels with him, then he will sit on his glorious throne. Before him will be gathered all the nations, and he will separate them one from another as a shepherd separates the sheep from the goats, and he will place the sheep at his right hand, but the goats at the left. Then the King will say to those at his right hand, 'Come, O blessed of my Father, inherit the kingdom prepared for you from the foundation of the world; for I was hungry and you gave me food, I was thirsty and you gave me drink, I was a stranger and you welcomed me, I was naked and you clothed me, I was sick and you visited me, I was in prison and you came to me.'

"Then the righteous will answer him, 'Lord, when did we see thee hungry and feed thee, or thirsty and give thee drink? And when did we see thee a stranger and welcome thee, or naked and clothe thee? And when did we see thee sick or in prison and visit thee?'

"And the King will answer them, 'Truly, I say to you, as you did it to one of the least of these my brethren, you did it to me.'"

This is the gospel of the Lord.

210.   Mark 2:1-12

A reading from the holy gospel according to Mark

Seeing their faith, Jesus said: your sins are forgiven

When Jesus returned to Capernaum after some days, it was reported that he was at home. And many were gathered together, so that there was no longer room for them, not even about the door; and he was preaching the word to them. And they came, bringing to him a paralytic carried by four men. And when they could not get near him because of the crowd, they removed the roof above him; and when they had made an opening, they let down the pallet on which the paralytic lay. And when Jesus saw their faith, he said to the paralytic, "My son, your sins are forgiven."

Now some of the scribes were sitting there questioning in their hearts, "Why does this man speak thus? It is blasphemy! Who can forgive sins but God alone?"

And immediately Jesus, perceiving in his spirit that they thus questioned within themselves, said to them, "Why do you question thus in your hearts? Which is easier, to say to the paralytic, 'Your sins are forgiven,' or to say, 'Rise, take up your pallet and walk'? But that you may know that the Son of man has authority on earth to forgive sins" — he said to the paralytic — "I say to you, rise, take up your pallet and go home."

And he rose, and immediately took up the pallet

and went out before them all; so that they were all
amazed and glorified God, saying, "We never saw
anything like this!"

This is the gospel of the Lord.

211.   Mark 4:35-41

A reading from the holy gospel according to Mark

Why are you so fearful? Why do you not have faith?

On that day, when evening had come, Jesus said
to his disciples, "Let us go across to the other
side." And leaving the crowd, they took him with
them, just as he was, in the boat. And other boats
were with him.

And a great storm of wind arose, and the waves
beat into the boat, so that the boat was already
filling. But he was in the stern, asleep on the
cushion; and they woke him and said to him,
"Teacher, do you not care if we perish?"

And he awoke and rebuked the wind, and said
to the sea, "Peace! Be still!" And the wind ceased,
and there was a great calm. He said to them,
"Why are you afraid? Have you no faith?"

And they were filled with awe, and said to one
another, "Who then is this that even wind and sea
obey him?"

This is the gospel of the Lord.

212.   Mark 10:46-52

A reading from the holy gospel according to Mark

Jesus, Son of David, have mercy on me

As Jesus was leaving Jericho with his disciples and a great multitude, Bartimaeus, a blind beggar, the son of Timaeus, was sitting by the roadside. And when he heard that it was Jesus of Nazareth, he began to cry out and say, "Jesus, Son of David, have mercy on me!" And many rebuked him, telling him to be silent; but he cried out all the more, "Son of David, have mercy on me!"

And Jesus stopped and said, "Call him."

And they called the blind man, saying to him, "Take heart; rise, he is calling you."

And throwing off his mantle he sprang up and came to Jesus. And Jesus said to him, "What do you want me to do for you?"

And the blind man said to him, "Master, let me receive my sight."

And Jesus said to him, "Go your way; your faith has made you well." And immediately he received his sight and followed him on the way.

This is the gospel of the Lord.

213.   Mark 16:15-20

The conclusion of the holy gospel according to Mark

He laid hands on the sick and they were cured

Jesus, appearing to the eleven, said to them, "Go into all the world and preach the gospel to the whole creation. He who believes and is baptized will be saved; but he who does not believe will be condemned. And these signs will accompany those who believe: in my name they will cast out demons; they will speak in new tongues; they will pick up serpents, and if they drink any deadly thing, it will not hurt them; they will lay their hands on the sick, and they will recover."

So then the Lord Jesus, after he had spoken to them, was taken up into heaven, and sat down at the right hand of God. And they went forth and preached everywhere, while the Lord worked with them and confirmed the message by the signs that attended it. Amen.

                    This is the gospel of the Lord.

214.   Luke 7:19-23

A reading from the holy gospel according to Luke

Go tell John what you have seen

John, calling to him two of his disciples, sent them to the Lord, saying, "Are you he who is to come, or shall we look for another?"

And when the men had come to him, they said, "John the Baptist has sent us to you, saying, 'Are you he who is to come, or shall we look for another?'"

In that hour he cured many of diseases and

plagues and evil spirits, and on many that were blind he bestowed sight. And he answered them, "Go and tell John what you have seen and heard: the blind receive their sight, the lame walk, lepers are cleansed, and the deaf hear, the dead are raised up, the poor have good news preached to them. And blessed is he who takes no offense at me."   **This is the gospel of the Lord.**

215.   Luke 10:5-6, 8-9

A reading from the holy gospel according to Luke

Heal the sick

Jesus told his disciples, "Whatever house you enter, first say, 'Peace be to this house!' And if a son of peace is there, your peace shall rest upon him; but if not, it shall return to you. Whenever you enter a town and they receive you, eat what is set before you; heal the sick in it and say to them, 'The kingdom of God has come near to you.'"

This is the gospel of the Lord.

216.   Luke 10:25-37

A reading from the holy gospel according to Luke

Who is my neighbor?

At that time, behold, a lawyer stood up to put Jesus to the test, saying, "Teacher, what shall I do to inherit eternal life?"

He said to him, "What is written in the law? How do you read?"

And he answered, "You shall love the Lord your God with all your heart, and with all your soul, and with all your strength, and with all your mind; and your neighbor as yourself."

And he said to him, "You have answered right; do this, and you will live."

But he, desiring to justify himself, said to Jesus, "And who is my neighbor?"

Jesus replied, "A man was going down from Jerusalem to Jericho, and he fell among robbers, who stripped him and beat him, and departed leaving him half dead. Now by chance a priest was going down that road; and when he saw him he passed by on the other side. So likewise a Levite, when he came to the place and saw him, passed by on the other side. But a Samaritan, as he journeyed, came to where he was; and when he saw him, he had compassion, and went to him and bound up his wounds, pouring on oil and wine; then he set him on his own beast and brought him to an inn, and took care of him. And the next day he took out two denarii and gave them to the innkeeper, saying, 'Take care of him; and whatever more you spend, I will repay you when I come back.' Which of these three, do you think, proved neighbor to the man who fell among the robbers?"

He said, "The one who showed mercy on him."

And Jesus said to him, "Go and do likewise."

This is the gospel of the Lord.

217.   Luke 11:5-13

A reading from the holy gospel according to Luke

Ask and it will be given to you

Jesus said to his disciples, "Which of you who has a friend will go to him at midnight and say to him, 'Friend, lend me three loaves; for a friend of mine has arrived on a journey, and I have nothing to set before him'; and he will answer from within, 'Do not bother me; the door is now shut, and my children are with me in bed; I cannot get up and give you anything'? I tell you, though he will not get up and give him anything because he is his friend, yet because of his importunity he will rise and give him whatever he needs. And I tell you, Ask, and it will be given you; seek, and you will find; knock, and it will be opened to you. For every one who asks receives, and he who seeks finds, and to him who knocks it will be opened. What father among you, if his son asks for a fish, will instead of a fish give him a serpent; or if he asks for an egg, will give him a scorpion? If you then, who are evil, know how to give good gifts to your children, how much more will the heavenly Father give the Holy Spirit to those who ask him!"

This is the gospel of the Lord.

218.   Luke 12:35-44

A reading from the holy gospel according to Luke

Happy are those whom the master
finds watching when he returns

Jesus said to his disciples, "Let your loins be girded and your lamps burning, and be like men who are waiting for their master to come home from the marriage feast, so that they may open to him at once when he comes and knocks. Blessed are those servants whom the master finds awake when he comes; truly, I say to you, he will gird himself and have them sit at table, and he will come and serve them. If he comes in the second watch, or in the third, and finds them so, blessed are those servants! But know this, that if the householder had known at what hour the thief was coming, he would have been awake and would not have left his house to be broken into. You also must be ready; for the Son of man is coming at an hour you do not expect."

Peter said, "Lord, are you telling this parable for us or for all?"

And the Lord said, "Who then is the faithful and wise steward, whom his master will set over his household, to give them their portion of food at the proper time? Blessed is that servant whom his master when he comes will find so doing. Truly I tell you, he will set him over all his possessions."

This is the gospel of the Lord.

219.   Luke 18:9-14

A reading from the holy gospel according to Luke

O God, be merciful to me, a sinner

Jesus told this parable to some who trusted in

themselves that they were righteous and despised others: "Two men went up into the temple to pray, one a Pharisee and the other a tax collector. The Pharisee stood and prayed thus with himself, 'God, I thank thee that I am not like other men, extortioners, unjust, adulterers, or even like this tax collector. I fast twice a week, I give tithes of all that I get.'

"But the tax collector, standing far off, would not even lift up his eyes to heaven, but beat his breast, saying 'God, be merciful to me a sinner!'

"I tell you, this man went down to his house justified rather than the other; for every one who exalts himself will be humbled, but he who humbles himself will be exalted."

This is the gospel of the Lord.

220.   (For the dying)   John 6:35-40

A reading from the holy gospel according to John

It is the will of my Father that what
he has given me will not perish

Jesus said to the crowds, "I am the bread of life; he who comes to me shall not hunger, and he who believes in me shall never thirst. But I said to you that you have seen me and yet do not believe. All that the Father gives me will come to me; and him who comes to me I will not cast out. For I have come down from heaven, not to do my own will, but the will of him who sent me; and this is the will of him who sent me, that I should lose nothing of all that he has given me, but raise it up at the last day. For this is the will of my Father, that every one who sees the Son and believes in him should have eternal life; and I will raise him up at the last day."

This is the gospel of the Lord.

221.   (For the dying)   John 6:53-58

A reading from the holy gospel according to John

He who eats this bread has eternal life

At that time Jesus said to them, "Truly, truly, I say to you, unless you eat the flesh of the Son of man and drink his blood, you have no life in you; he who eats my flesh and drinks my blood has eternal life, and I will raise him up at the last day. For my flesh is food indeed, and my blood is drink indeed. He who eats my flesh and drinks my blood abides in me, and I in him. As the living Father sent me, and I live because of the Father, so he who eats me will live because of me. This is the bread which came down from heaven, not such as the fathers ate and died; he who eats this bread will live for ever."

This is the gospel of the Lord.

222.   John 9:1-7

A reading from the holy gospel according to John

He has not sinned; it was to let
God's work show forth in him

As Jesus passed by, he saw a man blind from his birth. And his disciples asked him, "Rabbi, who sinned, this man or his parents, that he was born blind?"

Jesus answered, "It was not that this man sinned, or his parents, but that the works of God might be made manifest in him. We must work the works of him who sent me, while it is day; night comes, when no one can work. As long as I am in the world, I am the light of the world."

As he said this, he spat on the ground and made clay of the spittle and anointed the man's eyes with the clay, saying to him, "Go, wash in the pool of Siloam" (which means Sent). So he went and washed and came back seeing.

This is the gospel of the Lord.

223.   John 10:11-18

A reading from the holy gospel according to John

The good shepherd lays down his life for his sheep

Jesus said to his disciples, "I am the good shepherd. The good shepherd lays down his life for the sheep. He who is a hireling and not a shepherd, whose own the sheep are not, sees the wolf coming and leaves the sheep and flees; and the wolf snatches them and scatters them. He flees because he is a hireling and cares nothing for the sheep. I am the good shepherd; I know my own and my own know me, as the Father knows me and

I know the Father; and I lay down my life for the sheep. And I have other sheep, that are not of this fold; I must bring them also, and they will heed my voice. So there shall be one flock, one shepherd. For this reason the Father loves me, because I lay down my life, that I may take it again. No one takes it from me, but I lay it down of my own accord. I have power to lay it down, and I have power to take it again; this charge I have received from my Father."

This is the gospel of the Lord.

Readings from the Passion

224. If desired, readings may also be taken from the passion of the Lord as read on Passion Sunday (*Lectionary for Mass*, no. 38), Good Friday (*ibid.*, no. 903), or the following:

225.   Matthew 26:36-46

A reading from the holy gospel according to Matthew

If this cup cannot pass from me, then your will be done

Jesus went with his disciples to a place called Gethsemane, and he said to them, "Sit here, while I go yonder and pray." And taking with him Peter and the two sons of Zebedee, he began to be sorrowful and troubled. Then he said to them, "My soul is very sorrowful, even to death; remain here, and watch with me."

And going a little farther he fell on his face and prayed, "My Father, if it be possible, let this cup pass from me; nevertheless, not as I will, but as thou wilt."

And he came to the disciples and found them sleeping; and he said to Peter, "So, could you not watch with me one hour? Watch and pray that you may not enter into temptation; the spirit indeed is willing, but the flesh is weak."

Again, for the second time, he went away and prayed, "My Father, if this cannot pass unless I drink it, thy will be done." And again he came and found them sleeping, for their eyes were heavy.

So, leaving them again, he went away and prayed for the third time, saying the same words. Then he came to the disciples and said to them, "Are you still sleeping and taking your rest? Behold, the hour is at hand, and the Son of man is betrayed into the hands of sinners. Rise, let us be going; see, my betrayer is at hand."

This is the gospel of the Lord.

226.   Mark 15:33-39; 16:1-6

A reading from the holy gospel according to Mark

The death and resurrection of the Lord

When the sixth hour had come, there was darkness over the whole land until the ninth hour. And at the ninth hour Jesus cried with a loud voice,

Eloi, Eloi, lama sabachthani?" which means, "My God, my God, why hast thou forsaken me?"

And some of the bystanders hearing it said, "Behold, he is calling Elijah."

And one ran and, filling a sponge full of vinegar, put it on a reed and gave it to him to drink, saying, "Wait, let us see whether Elijah will come to take him down."

And Jesus uttered a loud cry, and breathed his last. And the curtain of the temple was torn in two, from top to bottom. And when the centurion, who stood facing him, saw that he thus breathed his last, he said, "Truly this man was the Son of God!"

And when the sabbath was past, Mary Magdalene, and Mary the mother of James, and Salome, bought spices, so that they might go and anoint him. And very early on the first day of the week they went to the tomb when the sun had risen. And they were saying to one another, "Who will roll away the stone for us from the door of the tomb?"

And looking up, they saw that the stone was rolled back; for it was very large. And entering the tomb, they saw a young man sitting on the right side, dressed in a white robe; and they were amazed.

And he said to them, "Do not be amazed; you seek Jesus of Nazareth, who was crucified. He has risen, he is not here; see the place where they laid him."

This is the gospel of the Lord.

227.   Luke 23:44-49; 24:1-5

A reading from the holy gospel according to Luke

The death and resurrection of the Lord

It was about the sixth hour, and there was darkness over the whole land until the ninth hour, while the sun's light failed; and the curtain of the temple was torn in two. Then Jesus, crying with a loud voice, said, "Father, into thy hands I commit my spirit!" And having said this he breathed his last.

Now when the centurion saw what had taken place, he praised God, and said, "Certainly this man was innocent!" And all the multitudes who assembled to see the sight, when they saw what had taken place, returned home beating their breasts. And all his acquaintances and the women who had followed him from Galilee stood at a distance and saw these things.

But on the first day of the week, at early dawn, they went to the tomb, taking the spices which they had prepared. And they found the stone rolled away from the tomb, but when they went in they did not find the body. While they were perplexed about this, behold, two men stood by them in dazzling apparel; and as they were frightened and bowed their faces to the ground, the men said to them, "Why do you seek the living among the dead? He is not here, but has risen."

This is the gospel of the Lord.

228.

A reading from the holy gospel according to Luke

*Was it not necessary for Christ to suffer
and so to enter into his glory?*

On the first day of the week two of the disciples of Jesus were going to a village named Emmaus, about seven miles from Jerusalem, and talking with each other about all these things that had happened. While they were talking and discussing together, Jesus himself drew near and went with them. But their eyes were kept from recognizing him. And he said to them, "What is this conversation which you are holding with each other as you walk?"

And they stood still, looking sad. Then one of them, named Cleopas, answered him, "Are you the only visitor to Jerusalem who does not know the things that have happened there in these days?"

And he said to them, "What things?"

And they said to him, "Concerning Jesus of Nazareth, who was a prophet mighty in deed and word before God and all the people, and how our chief priests and rulers delivered him up to be condemned to death, and crucified him. But we had hoped that he was the one to redeem Israel. Yes, and besides all this, it is now the third day since this happened. Moreover, some women of our company amazed us. They were at the tomb early in the morning and did not find his body; and they came back saying that they had even seen a vision of angels, who said that he was alive. Some of those who were with us went to the tomb, and found it just as the women had said; but him they did not see."

And he said to them, "O foolish men, and slow of heart to believe all that the prophets have spoken! Was it not necessary that the Christ should suffer these things and enter into his glory?" And beginning with Moses and all the prophets, he interpreted to them in all the scriptures the things concerning himself.

So they drew near to the village to which they were going. He appeared to be going further, but they constrained him, saying, "Stay with us, for it is toward evening and the day is now far spent." So he went in to stay with them. When he was at table with them, he took the bread and blessed, and broke it, and gave it to them. And their eyes were opened and they recognized him; and he vanished out of their sight. They said to each other, "Did not our hearts burn within us while he talked to us on the road, while he opened to us the scriptures?"

And they rose that same hour and returned to Jerusalem; and they found the eleven gathered together and those who were with them, who said, "The Lord has risen indeed, and has appeared to Simon!" Then they told what had happened on the road, and how he was known to them in the breaking of the bread.

This is the gospel of the Lord.

229.   John 20:1-10

A reading from the holy gospel according to John

He saw and he believed

On the first day of the week Mary Magdalene came to the tomb early, while it was still dark, and saw that the stone had been taken away from the tomb. So she ran, and went to Simon Peter and the other disciple, the one whom Jesus loved, and said to them, "They have taken the Lord out of the tomb, and we do not know where they have laid him."

Peter then came out with the other disciple, and they went toward the tomb. They both ran, but the other disciple outran Peter and reached the tomb first; and stooping to look in, he saw the linen cloths lying there, but he did not go in. Then Simon Peter came, following him, and went into the tomb; he saw the linen cloths lying, and the napkin, which had been on his head, not lying with the linen cloths but rolled up in a place by itself. Then the other disciple, who reached the tomb first, also went in, and he saw and believed; for as yet they did not know the scripture, that he must rise from the dead. Then the disciples went back to their homes.

This is the gospel of the Lord.

II. FORMS OF GREETING

230.

℣. **The grace of our Lord Jesus Christ and the love of God and the fellowship of the Holy Spirit be with you all.**

℟. **And also with you.**

231.

℣. **The grace and peace of God our Father and the Lord Jesus Christ be with you.**

℟. **Blessed be God the Father of our Lord Jesus Christ.**

Or:

℟. **And also with you.**

III. FORMS OF THE PENITENTIAL RITE

232. The priest invites the people to repent of their sins:

My brothers and sisters, to prepare ourselves for this celebration, let us call to mind our sins.

After a brief silence, the priest says:

**Lord, we have sinned against you:
Lord, have mercy.**

All answer: **Lord, have mercy.**

Priest: **Lord, show us your mercy and love.**

All answer: **And grant us your salvation.**

The priest concludes:

**May almighty God have mercy on us,
forgive us our sins,
and bring us to everlasting life.**

All answer: **Amen.**

233. The priest invites the people to repent of their sins:

My brothers and sisters, to prepare ourselves for this celebration, let us call to mind our sins.

After a brief silence, the priest or one of the others present says the following or other invocations with the Kyrie:

**You brought us to salvation by your paschal mystery:
Lord, have mercy.**

All answer: **Lord, have mercy.**

Priest: **You renew us by the wonders of your passion:
Christ, have mercy.**

All answer: **Christ, have mercy.**

Priest: **You make us sharers in your paschal sacrifice
by our partaking of your body:
Lord, have mercy.**

All answer: **Lord, have mercy.**

The priest concludes:

**May almighty God have mercy on us,
forgive us our sins,
and bring us to everlasting life.**

All answer: **Amen.**

IV. PRAYERS AFTER COMMUNION

234.

**Father,
you brought to completion
the work of our redemption
through the paschal mystery of Christ your Son.
May we who faithfully proclaim
his death and resurrection
in these sacramental signs
experience the constant growth of your salvation
  in our lives.**

We ask this through Christ our Lord.

235.

**God our Father,
you give us a share in the one bread and the one
  cup.
and make us one in Christ.
May our lives bring your salvation and joy
to all the world.**

We ask this through Christ our Lord.

236.

Lord,
in the eucharist we share today
you renew our life.
Through your Spirit,
make your life grow strong within us
and keep us faithful to you.

We ask this in the name of Jesus the Lord.

V. BLESSINGS

237.

May the Lord Jesus Christ be with you to protect you.

℟. **Amen.**

May he go before you to guide you and stand behind you to give you strength.

℟. **Amen.**

May he look upon you, to keep you and bless you.

℟. **Amen.**

[And may almighty God,
the Father, and the Son, ✝ and the Holy Spirit,
bless you all.

℟. **Amen.**]

238.

May the blessing of almighty God,

the Father, and the Son, ✝ and the Holy Spirit,
come upon you and remain with you for ever.

℟. Amen.

VI. FOR THE ANOINTING OF THE SICK

239.   Opening prayer of the rite of anointing:

This prayer may take the place of the instruction
at the beginning of the anointing of the sick.

Lord God,
you have told us through your apostle James:
"Is there anyone sick among you?
Let him call for the elders of the Church,
and let them pray over him
and anoint him in the name of the Lord.
This prayer, made in faith, will save the sick man.
The Lord will restore his health,
and if he has committed any sins,
they will be forgiven."

Gathered here in your name,
we ask you to listen to the prayer
   we make in faith:
in your love and kindness,
protect our brother (sister) N. in his (her)
   illness
[and all the sick here present].
Lead us all to the peace and joy of your kingdom
where you live for ever and ever.

℟. Amen.

240.   Other litanies for use before the anointing:

You bore our weakness and carried our sorrow:
Lord, have mercy.

℟. **Lord, have mercy.**

You felt compassion for the crowd,
and went among them doing good and healing the
  sick:
Christ, have mercy.

℟. **Christ, have mercy.**

You commanded the apostles
to lay their hands on the sick in your name:
Lord, have mercy.

℟. **Lord, have mercy.**

   241.

Let us pray to the Lord for our sick brother (sister)
and for all those dedicated to serving and caring
for him (her). Look kindly on our sick brother (sis-
ter).

℟. **Lord, hear our prayer.**

Give new strength to his (her) body and mind.

℟. **Lord, hear our prayer.**

Ease our brother's (sister's) sufferings.

℟. **Lord, hear our prayer.**

Free him (her) from sin and temptation.

℟. **Lord, hear our prayer.**

Sustain all the sick with your power.

℟. **Lord, hear our prayer.**

Assist all who care for the sick.

℟. **Lord, hear our prayer.**

**Give life and health to our brother (sister),
on whom we lay our hands in your name.**

℟. **Lord, hear our prayer.**

242.   Another blessing of the oil for the sick.

**Praise to you, almighty God and Father.
You sent your Son to live among us
and bring us salvation.**

℟. **Blessed be God.**

**Praise to you, Lord Jesus Christ,
the Father's only Son.
You humbled yourself to share in our humanity,
  and desired to cure all our illnesses.**

℟. **Blessed be God.**

**Praise to you, God the Holy Spirit, the Consoler.
You heal our sickness with your mighty power.**

℟. **Blessed be God.**

**Lord,
mercifully listen to our prayers
and bless this oil intended to ease the sufferings
  of your people.**

May those for whom we pray in faith
and who are anointed with this holy oil,
be freed from the illness that afflicts them.

We ask this through Christ our Lord.

℟. Amen.

Prayers after Anointing

243.   When the illness is the result of advanced
age.

Lord,
look kindly on our brother (sister)
who has grown weak under the burden of his (her)
**   years.**
In this holy anointing
he (she) asks for the grace of health in body and
**   soul.**
By the power of your Holy Spirit,
make him (her) firm in faith and sure in hope,
so that his (her) cheerful patience
may reveal your love to us.

We ask this through Christ our Lord.

℟. **Amen.**

244.   When the sick person is in great danger.

Lord Jesus Christ,
you took our weakness on yourself
and bore our sufferings in your passion and death.
Hear this prayer for our suffering brother (sister) N.
You are his (her) Redeemer:

strengthen his (her) hope for salvation
and in your kindness sustain him (her)
in body and soul.

You live and reign for ever and ever.

℞. Amen.

245. When anointing and viaticum are given
together.

Lord God, merciful Father, comforter of the suffering,
look kindly on your son (daughter) N., who trusts
in you.
May this anointing ease his (her) sufferings,
and may the food he (she) has received for his
(her) journey,
the body and blood of your Son Jesus Christ,
refresh him (her) and lead him (her) to life.

We ask this through Christ our Lord.

℞. Amen.

246. For those about to die.

Lord God, loving Father,
you are the source of all goodness and love,
and you never refuse forgiveness
to those who are sorry for their sins.
Have mercy on your son (daughter) N.,
who is about to return to you.
May this holy anointing
and our prayer made in faith assist him (her):

relieve his (her) pain, in body and soul,
forgive all his (her) sins,
and strengthen him (her) with your loving
    protection.

We ask this, Father, through your Son Jesus Christ,
who conquered death
and opened for us the way to eternal life,
and who lives and reigns for ever and ever.

℞. Amen.

VII. MASS FOR VIATICUM

Biblical Readings

First Reading

247.   1 Kings 19:4-8

A reading from the first book of Kings

*Strengthened by that food,
he walked to the mountain of God*

**Elijah went a day's journey into the wilderness,
and came and sat down under a broom tree; and
he asked that he might die, saying, "It is enough;
now, O Lord, take away my life; for I am no better
than my fathers." And he lay down and slept under
a broom tree; and behold, an angel touched him,
and said to him, "Arise and eat." And he looked
and behold, there was at his head a cake baked
on hot stones and a jar of water. And he ate and**

drank, and lay down again. And the angel of the Lord came again a second time, and touched him, and said, "Arise and eat, else the journey will be too great for you." And he arose, and ate and drank, and went in the strength of that food forty days and forty nights to Horeb the mount of God.

This is the Word of the Lord.

248.   1 Corinthians 11:23-26

A reading from the first letter of Paul to the Corinthians

When you eat this bread and drink this cup,
you proclaim the death of the Lord

I received from the Lord what I also delivered to you, that the Lord Jesus on the night when he was betrayed took bread, and when he had given thanks, he broke it, and said, "This is my body which is for you. Do this in remembrance of me." In the same way also the cup, after supper, saying, "This cup is the new covenant in my blood. Do this, as often as you drink it, in remembrance of me." For as often as you eat this bread and drink the cup, you proclaim the Lord's death until he comes.   **This is the Word of the Lord.**

Responsorial Psalm

249.   Psalm 23:1-3a, 3b-4, 5, 6

℟. (4a) Though I walk in the valley of darkness, I fear no evil, for you are with me.

or **(1) The Lord is my shepherd; there is nothing I shall want.**

**The Lord is my shepherd, I shall not want;
     he makes me lie down in green pastures.
He leads me beside still waters;
     he restores my soul.**

℟. **Though . . . or The Lord . . .**

**He leads me in paths of righteousness
     for his name's sake.
Even though I walk through the valley of the
     shadow of death,
     I fear no evil;
for thou art with me;
     thy rod and thy staff, they comfort me.**

℟. **Though . . . or The Lord . . .**

**Thou preparest a table before me
     in the presence of my enemies;
thou anointest my head with oil,
     my cup overflows.**

℟. **Though . . . or The Lord . . .**

**Surely goodness and mercy shall follow me
     all the days of my life;
and I shall dwell in the house of the Lord
     for ever.**

℟. **Though . . . or The Lord . . .**

250.   Psalm 34:1-2, 3-4, 5-6, 9-10

℟. **(9a) Taste and see the goodness of the Lord.**

I will bless the Lord at all times;
  his praise shall continually be in my mouth.
My soul makes its boast in the Lord;
  let the afflicted hear and be glad.

℟. Taste and see the goodness of the Lord.

O magnify the Lord with me,
  and let us exalt his name together!
I sought the Lord, and he answered me,
  and delivered me from all my fears.

℟. Taste and see the goodness of the Lord.

Look to him, and be radiant;
  so your faces shall never be ashamed.
This poor man cried, and the Lord heard him,
  and saved him out of all his troubles.

℟. Taste and see the goodness of the Lord.

O fear the Lord, you his saints,
  for those who fear him have no want!
The young lions suffer want and hunger;
  but those who seek the Lord lack no good
    thing.

℟. Taste and see the goodness of the Lord.

251.   Psalm 42:1, 2, 4; Psalm 43:3, 4, 5

℟. (Psalm 42:2) My soul is thirsting for the living
  God; when shall I see him face to face?

As a hart longs
  for flowing streams,

so longs my soul
   for thee, O God.

℟. My soul is thirsting for the living God; when
   shall I see him face to face?

My soul thirsts for God,
   for the living God.
When shall I come and behold
   the face of God?

℟. My soul is thirsting for the living God; when
   shall I see him face to face?

These things I remember,
   as I pour out my soul:
how I went with the throng,
   and led them in procession to the house of
     God,
with glad shouts and songs of thanksgiving,
   a multitude keeping festival.

℟. My soul is thirsting for the living God; when
   shall I see him face to face?

Oh send out thy light and thy truth;
   let them lead me,
let them bring me to thy holy hill
   and to thy dwelling!

℟. My soul is thirsting for the living God; when
   shall I see him face to face?

Then I will go to the altar of God,
   to God my exceeding joy;

and I will praise thee with the lyre,
   O God, my God.

℟. My soul is thirsting for the living God; when
   shall I see him face to face?

Why are you cast down, O my soul,
   and why are you disquieted within me?
Hope in God; for I shall again praise him,
   my help and my God.

℟. My soul is thirsting for the living God; when
   shall I see him face to face?

252.   Psalm 116:12-13, 15 and 16bc, 17-18

℟. **(Psalm 116:9) I will walk in the presence of the
   Lord, in the land of the living.**
   or **(Psalm 116:13) I will take the cup of salvation and call on the name of the Lord.**
   or **Alleluia.**

What shall I render to the Lord
   for all his bounty to me?
I will lift up the cup of salvation
   and call on the name of the Lord.

℟. **I will walk in the presence of the Lord, in the
   land of the living.**
   or **I will take the cup of salvation and call on the
   name of the Lord.**
   or **Alleluia.**

Precious in the sight of the Lord
   is the death of his saints.

I am thy servant, the son of thy handmaid.
    Thou hast loosed my bonds.

℟. I will walk in the presence of the Lord, in the
    land of the living.
    or I will take the cup of salvation and call on the
    name of the Lord.
    or **Alleluia.**

I will offer to thee the sacrifice of thanksgiving
    and call on the name of the Lord.
I will pay my vows to the Lord
    in the presence of all his people.

℟. I will walk in the presence of the Lord, in the
    land of the living.
    or I will take the cup of salvation and call on the
    name of the Lord.
    or **Alleluia.**

Alleluia Verse and Verse before the Gospel

253.   John 6:51

I am the living bread from heaven, says the Lord;
if anyone eats this bread, he will live for ever.

254.   John 6:54

He who eats my flesh and drinks my blood
has eternal life, says the Lord;
and I will raise him up on the last day.

255.   John 10:9

I am the gate, says the Lord;
he who enters through me will be safe and find
    pasture.

256.   John 11:25; 14:6

I am the resurrection and the life, says the Lord: no one comes to the Father except by me.

Gospel

257.   John 6:41-51a

A reading from the holy gospel according to John

I am the bread of life that comes down from heaven

The Jews murmured at Jesus because he said, "I am the bread which came down from heaven."

They said, "Is not this Jesus, the son of Joseph, whose father and mother we know? How does he now say, 'I have come down from heaven'?"

Jesus answered them, "Do not murmur among yourselves. No one can come to me unless the Father who sent me draws him; and I will raise him up at the last day. It is written in the prophets, 'And they shall all be taught by God.' Every one who has heard and learned from the Father comes to me. Not that any one has seen the Father except him who is from God; he has seen the Father. Truly, truly, I say to you, he who believes has eternal life. I am the bread of life. Your fathers ate the manna in the wilderness, and they died. This is the bread which comes down from heaven, that a man may eat of it and not die. I am the living bread

which came down from heaven; if any one eats of this bread, he will live for ever."

> This is the gospel of the Lord.

258.   John 6:51-58

A reading from the holy gospel according to John

If anyone eats this bread he will live for ever and I will raise him up on the last day

Jesus said to the crowds of the Jews, "I am the living bread which came down from heaven; if any one eats of this bread, he will live for ever; and the bread which I shall give for the life of the world is my flesh."

The Jews then disputed among themselves, saying, "How can this man give us his flesh to eat?"

So Jesus said to them, "Truly, truly, I say to you, unless you eat the flesh of the Son of man and drink his blood, you have no life in you; he who eats my flesh and drinks my blood has eternal life, and I will raise him up at the last day. For my flesh is food indeed, and my blood is drink indeed. He who eats my flesh and drinks my blood abides in me, and I in him. As the living Father sent me, and I live because of the Father, so he who eats me will live because of me. This is the bread which came down from heaven, not such as the fathers ate and died; he who eats this bread will live for ever."

> This is the gospel of the Lord.

259.   Another prayer after viaticum:

Lord,
you are the source of eternal health
for those who believe in you.
May our brother (sister) N.,
who has been refreshed with food and drink from
   heaven,
safely reach your kingdom of light and life.

We ask this through Christ our Lord.

℟. Amen.